THE ANTI-BURNOUT JOURNAL

A 12-week multi-platform wellness planner
for self-care and stress relief

Bex Spiller

DAVID & CHARLES

www.davidandcharles.com

Contents

WELCOME! A FEW SECRETS I WANT TO SHARE................................4

HOW TO USE THIS JOURNAL AND RESOURCES 6

BRAIN DUMPING 8

WEEK ONE: SET YOUR INTENTIONS 10

WEEK TWO: CHANGE YOUR HABITS 30

WEEK THREE: BE GRATEFUL 50

WEEK FOUR: MOVE YOUR BODY 70

WEEK FIVE: BECOME MINDFUL 90

WEEK SIX: UNPLUG YOURSELF..110

WEEK SEVEN: BE KIND 130

WEEK EIGHT: TRY MEDITATION.....................................150

WEEK NINE: FUEL YOUR BODY AND MIND 170

WEEK TEN: PRACTISE YOGA 190

WEEK ELEVEN: GET MORE SLEEP 210

WEEK TWELVE: CELEBRATE YOUR SUCCESS 230

YOU DID IT! SOME FINAL NOTES FROM BEX 250

MY FINAL REFLECTION LETTER......................................251

ABOUT BEX...254

ACKNOWLEDGEMENTS..254

ABOUT THE ANTI-BURNOUT CLUB................................255

Welcome! A Few Secrets I Want to Share...

Hello and welcome to *The Anti-Burnout Journal*! My name is Bex and I'm going to be taking you through this journey for the next 12 weeks. Before you dig in, however, I wanted to let you in on a few little secrets...

SECRET #1 – I'M A JOURNAL ADDICT

The first secret is that I've been a journal and diary addict for as long as I can remember. I have more journals, notebooks and diaries in my house than your local stationery store – fact! I've always bought a couple of different journals each year because I could never find anything that covered all of the areas that I wanted! So, when the chance came to create my very own journal I jumped at it. I've used all of my knowledge and experience with all those different journals to, hopefully, create something that will help you stay on track and improve key aspects of your health and well-being. I can finally stop buying 23 new ones a year!

SECRET #2 – I'M STILL LEARNING

After running a successful content agency for nearly 10 years, I tried to juggle so much at once it became overwhelming. I burnt out bad, had high blood pressure, and my cortisol (stress hormone) levels were through the roof. I set up The Anti-Burnout Club (The ABC) in January 2021 after a long time studying various areas of mindfulness and holistic well-being, but that doesn't mean I have all of the answers. In fact, one of the best things about The ABC is that I get to learn every single day: from our teachers, the members, from continuing my studies, and even writing this journal.

SECRET #3 – THERE IS NO PERFECT

With this in mind, it's time to let go of the strive for perfection! As a self-confessed perfectionist and a bit of a control freak, understanding this was the key to my growth. There will be days you forget to fill in your journal, weeks you have to put things on hold, and it may take longer than 12 weeks to finish everything put together here. But that is OKAY. The more you beat yourself up about missing a day, the harder it will be to keep going. Don't worry, I'll cover this more in one of your first lessons.

SECRET #4 – IT TAKES TIME

Another lesson you'll quickly learn throughout this journal is that slow and steady wins the race. As mentioned, I'm still learning how to find the perfect balance. There are some days I still don't want to get out of bed, or get in front of the camera to film a lesson, or eat healthy and nutritious food, or move my body. However, I make sure that I focus on one small step at a time and build upon these to create the best, most balanced version of myself. This journal is for 12 weeks, but it may take longer to achieve everything you want to achieve. In fact, it should take longer! As you get towards the end, I'll give you some great tips for keeping up the momentum with the changes you have made.

SECRET #5 – GET YOUR MONEY'S WORTH, BUT DON'T GET OVERWHELMED!

One of my biggest aims has always been to make self-care as accessible for as many people as possible, which is why there are so many extra resources that come with this journal. Each week, alongside the written lessons, you'll find articles, explainer videos, classes and recipes to complement your learning. When and where you can, make the most of these! You'll always have access to them, so if it means returning to any that you have missed at the end of the 12 weeks then do so.

The key is not to get information overload and feel overwhelmed. Only you know how much spare time you have to work on your Anti-Burnout journey each week. If you only have time to read the basics and fill in your planner, then do that. If you have some free time to expand your learning with the resources, then do that. Just ensure that it works for you, and remember you can come back to the extra resources at any time.

Read through the next few pages carefully to ensure that you know how best to use the journal and the resources too.

Finally, I just want to give you the warmest welcome and wish you the best of luck on this journey. Chances are, if you've bought this journal, then you know you want to make some real changes in your life. Perhaps you're feeling stressed, burnt out, anxious or low – and I know what that's like, I've been there countless times. I genuinely hope that the next 12 weeks create some truly positive changes for you, and that you reach the end of this journal with more balance and happiness.

If there is anything you ever need, always know you can reach out to me through the website, via email, or on social media. I love connecting with you all, so do come and say hi!

For now, enjoy and take care,

Bex x

How to Use This Journal and Resources

Whether this is your first-ever journal or your 4000th, please do read through the next couple of pages before you get started. Going through these instructions will ensure you can get the most out of your journal and the resources that come with it. As I mentioned in the introduction, if you ever get stuck or need some help, then please do feel free to reach out through the website, via email or on social media.

It's important to note that this journal is undated, so you can start whenever you'd like – there's space to fill in your own dates! That means you can also stop and come back to the journal at your own pace (remember the secrets I shared with you earlier).

Let's go through each of the different sections so you can make the most of *The Anti-Burnout Journal*, and to make sure you can access the extra online resources too.

WEEKLY LESSONS

First up, you will find a new lesson at the beginning of each week – 12 in total. Here I'll explain a little bit about what our focus is for the week and why it's an important topic. These lessons are packed full of tips and tricks to get the most out of each week, so dedicate some time to going through each one. I've tried to keep them down to around 10-15 minutes of work each week, reading the lesson and filling in your weekly planner – I don't want anyone feeling overwhelmed!

WEEKLY PLANNER

Once you have read each lesson, you'll have a weekly planner to fill in. Here you'll find prompts to get the most out of each week, usually in the form of questions or asking you to list information, and sometimes inviting you to come back and fill something in throughout the week. Remember, reading the weekly lesson and filling in the weekly planner shouldn't take much more than 10-15 minutes. However, the extra online resources provided at the end of the weekly planner will take a little more time, so review these as and when you can.

There is also space to fill in one big goal for the week, anything else you'd like to achieve, important things to remember, and for making notes.

DAILY PLANNER

Each day you have a daily planner, with one page for planning and one for an end of day check-in. You'll find space for your daily intention (we'll cover this in Week 1), top 3 priorities, a habit tracker (explored in Week 2), and your schedule.

For the end of day check-in, you can fill in what went well that day, what you can improve on tomorrow, three things you're grateful for, and mark where your mood is on the scale. Please spend 5 minutes or so checking in at the end of each day, as it's really important to measure progress!

You will find that the weekend pages are slightly different, combining priorities, gratitudes and mood tracker to cover both Saturday and Sunday.

END OF WEEK CHECK-INS

At the end of each week, we have another check-in to see how the lesson has gone. Here you will find questions relating to the topic of the lesson, as well as some general questions to celebrate your achievements, review what made you happy, and preview how you can make next week amazing.

Again, it's important to have that reflection time at the end of the week, so spend 10-15 minutes filling that in before planning the next week.

EXTRA ONLINE RESOURCES

For the days when you have a little more time or want to learn further, you will find the extra online resources extremely helpful! We have articles, video lessons with me, classes from The Anti-Burnout Club teachers, recipes, and so much more for you to take advantage of. I wanted this journal to be a complete multi-platform experience, so you can enjoy the traditional pen and paper tasks alongside a range of digital tools.

To make sure you get access to these, head to **https://theantiburnoutclub.com/journal**, fill in your name, email address, and the following code: **ABCJLU**

This will sign you up for an exclusive section of the site just for journal users! Each week, a new section will unlock with the resources for that lesson. You'll also have unlimited access to these resources, so you can come back and use them time and time again. Access to this area of the site is included in the price of the journal, so you don't need to pay any extra.

THE BRAIN DUMP

We're about to head into the brain dump section. Over the page, I'll explain a little bit about the joys of brain dumping and give you a full page for your own. Some people prefer doing the main bulk of their brain dump on scrap paper and then transferring it into their journal once it has been organised.

You can also use the notes section in the weekly planner to jot down brain dumps each week. Find a method that works for you, but trust me when I say, brain dumping will change your life...

Brain Dumping

One of my favourite ways to release stress and feel less overwhelmed is the humble brain dump – so I couldn't create a journal without including space for yours! I'll quickly walk you through how to brain dump and then leave you with a page for your own.

WHAT IS A BRAIN DUMP?

A brain dump is effectively a way of getting all of your thoughts out of your head and onto paper. Our brains aren't designed to carry everything in them at once; from grandma's birthday to adding bread to the shopping list – and not forgetting to take out the bins either. Brain dumping allows us to clear space in our minds and untangle our thoughts.

It's also an extremely powerful way to rid yourself of stress and overwhelming anxiety. Getting all of those thoughts out of your head lets you see what's really important and what can be ditched forever!

HOW TO BRAIN DUMP

There are plenty of different ways to brain dump, but I like to keep it simple. Start with a scrap piece of paper and use it to jot down anything that comes to mind – and I mean anything. Reminders, appointments, things you can't forget, worries, tasks, get it all out onto that piece of paper.

Now, take a look and see what can be added somewhere useful – appointments in calendars, bits to buy on a shopping list, and so on. You can also categorise any tasks into different areas such as home, work, family, etc. Spend a little bit of time sorting through and putting anything that needs to be actioned somewhere safe. You can also use the page opposite for this sorting exercise.

Finally, look at anything that's taking up brain space that doesn't deserve it. The ruminating thoughts, worries, intrusive ideas. Now, let them go! Cross them off. Write them on another piece of paper and rip them up. Get rid! They do not deserve to be taking up so much valuable space in your mind.

You have space in your weekly planner for notes and I'd recommend popping down any smaller brain dumps there before starting a new week. You can then add anything useful to your schedule and get rid of anything that's wasting brain space!

Most of all, enjoy it! It feels amazing to get all of these thoughts out of our minds for good.

My Brain Dump

Week One
Set Your Intentions

Let's start at the very beginning by setting intentions! The right intentions can help you feel focused, motivated and ensure you enjoy every step of this exciting new journey.

Setting Your Intentions

When we start something new, like this journal, we're often excited about what's to come. However, as time goes on, we can lose that motivation and need something to keep us going. This is where setting intentions comes in. The right intentions can help us find focus, propel us towards achieving our goals, and allow us to enjoy the journey. In your Week 1 online resources, you'll find an 'Introduction to Intentions' video where I explain what intentions are and why they're so useful. Once you've got to grips with the basics, come back and let's start planning your first week!

ASK YOURSELF THIS

Before we get stuck into learning methods to improve well-being, it's important to start by setting intentions and asking ourselves some questions:

* Why did I buy this journal?

* What do I want to gain from it?

* How do I want to feel at the end of the 12 weeks?

* What could hold me back from achieving my intentions?

* What can I put in place to overcome the hurdles before they arise?

You likely already had certain intentions in mind when you first picked up this journal. Perhaps you wanted to feel more relaxed, create a better work-life balance, or just to improve your overall well-being. Think about your reasons for investing in this journal and how you want to feel at the end of this 12-week journey.

It's also important to spend a little bit of time thinking about what may hold you back and how you can get over any future hurdles. By getting one step ahead of these potential issues, you can plan and prepare for them before they arise.

In your planner for Week 1, you'll see some space to answer these questions and start thinking about your initial reasons for being here right now. Set a timer for 60 seconds and answer each question with your gut feeling. The first thing that pops into your head is generally how you truly feel, so don't be afraid to jot that down.

TURNING YOUR ANSWERS INTO INTENTIONS

Once you have answered the questions, it's time to turn these into intentions. To do this, we need to focus on the three Ps:

Personal: These intentions have to be personal to us and what we want from life. Don't set intentions that are based on other people's opinions of you or what you think other people might want from you. Set your intentions for you and you alone.

Positive: If we set an intention to 'not be stressed today' then what's the one word we're saying to ourselves often? Stressed. We're setting a negative tone from the outset. So, frame it positively. For example, 'I intend to feel calm and relaxed today'.

Present: Intentions focus on the present and not the future. The joy of intentions is focusing on the here and now, so ensure that yours reflect this. The future is for goals and I'll talk a little bit about that in the next section.

Finally, think about those hurdles you wrote down when answering the questions. Can you set an intention to combat those? If you think that finding the time is going to be an issue, then make this one of your intentions: 'I intend to make time for myself and my journal today'.

USING INTENTIONS TO ACHIEVE BIG GOALS

As mentioned, intentions are very much about the present moment and how we want to feel and be right now. When we look towards the future, we may think about bigger goals that the setting of these intentions will enable us to achieve. Throughout this journal, you'll find spaces to record goals that you want to achieve each day and each week. Use your daily intentions to help shape those goals and really propel yourself towards success.

In your Week 1 resources online, you'll find a helpful guide to the differences between goals and intentions, and how to use your intentions to set your long-term goals.

VISUALISING YOUR SUCCESS

Now we have our intentions in place, it's time to visualise what life will be like for us at the end of these 12 weeks. Will we have more free time? Will we feel calmer and more relaxed? The final resource on the site for this week is a visualisation that will help us picture what life will be like for us by the end of this exciting journey.

While it's important to use this visualisation in Week 1, to help set those intentions, there's an even more important time to use it... when you're struggling! If you feel as though you're losing motivation or want to throw in the towel, come back to this visualisation technique and remember why you wanted this.

Make these intentions part of your morning routine and don't be afraid to upgrade or change them at any time. Good luck!

ONLINE RESOURCES FOR WEEK 1

* Video: Introduction to intentions (what are they, why set them?)

* Article: The difference between goals and intentions (and why/ how to set both)

* Video: Visualising our intentions and what we want to gain by the end of the 12 weeks

www.theantiburnoutclub.com/journal

Week One: Set Your Intentions

Set a timer for 60 seconds for each question below. Write down your gut feeling for each answer.

1. Why did I buy this journal?

....

2. What do I want to gain from it?

....

3. How do I want to feel at the end of the 12 weeks?

....

4. What could hold me back from achieving my intentions?

....

5. What can I put in place to overcome the hurdles before they arise?

....

Using the answers to your questions, set three intentions below. Remember to make then Personal, Positive and Present.

✱ ....

✱ ....

✱ ....

Remember to check in with your intentions daily. You can also come back to this lesson and the visualisation if you're struggling or need a reminder of why you're on the journey!

WEEK COMMENCING:

ONE BIG GOAL FOR THE WEEK:

THIS WEEK WILL BE AMAZING IF I ALSO ACHIEVE...

1. ....
   ....

2. ....
   ....

3. ....
   ....

4. ....
   ....

5. ....
   ....

IMPORTANT THINGS TO REMEMBER THIS WEEK:

Monday:

Tuesday:

Wednesday:

Thursday:

Friday:

Saturday:

Sunday:

NOTES FOR THIS WEEK:

Monday

DATE:

TOP 3 PRIORITIES:

1. ....
   ....
   ....

2. ....
   ....
   ....

3. ....
   ....
   ....

HABIT TRACKER:

☐ ....
☐ ....
☐ ....
☐ ....
☐ ....

DAILY INTENTION:

8am: ....
9am: ....
10am: ....
11am: ....
12pm: ....
1pm: ....
2pm: ....
3pm: ....
4pm: ....
5pm: ....
6pm: ....
7pm: ....
8pm: ....
9pm: ....
10pm: ....

"Setting goals is the first step in turning the invisible into the visible."

TONY ROBBINS

End of day check-in

WHAT WENT WELL TODAY?

HOW CAN I IMPROVE TOMORROW?

THREE THINGS I AM GRATEFUL FOR TODAY

TODAY I'VE FELT...

Tuesday

DATE:

TOP 3 PRIORITIES:

1. ....
....
....

2. ....
....
....

3. ....
....
....

HABIT TRACKER:

- ☐ ....
- ☐ ....
- ☐ ....
- ☐ ....
- ☐ ....

DAILY INTENTION:

8am: ....
9am: ....
10am: ....
11am: ....
12pm: ....
1pm: ....
2pm: ....
3pm: ....
4pm: ....
5pm: ....
6pm: ....
7pm: ....
8pm: ....
9pm: ....
10pm: ....

*" Success is liking yourself,
liking what you do, and
liking how you do it."*

MAYA ANGELOU

End of day check-in

WHAT WENT WELL TODAY?

HOW CAN I IMPROVE TOMORROW?

THREE THINGS I AM GRATEFUL FOR TODAY

TODAY I'VE FELT...

Wednesday

DATE:

DAILY INTENTION:

TOP 3 PRIORITIES:

1. ....

....

....

2. ....

....

....

3. ....

....

....

HABIT TRACKER:

☐ ....

☐ ....

☐ ....

☐ ....

☐ ....

8am: ....

9am: ....

10am: ....

11am: ....

12pm: ....

1pm: ....

2pm: ....

3pm: ....

4pm: ....

5pm: ....

6pm: ....

7pm: ....

8pm: ....

9pm: ....

10pm: ....

" If you want to live a happy life, tie it to a goal, not to people or things."

ALBERT EINSTEIN

End of day check-in

WHAT WENT WELL TODAY?

HOW CAN I IMPROVE TOMORROW?

THREE THINGS I AM GRATEFUL FOR TODAY

TODAY I'VE FELT...

Thursday

DATE:

DAILY INTENTION:

TOP 3 PRIORITIES:

1. ....
   ....
   ....

2. ....
   ....
   ....

3. ....
   ....
   ....

WEEK ONE | 22

HABIT TRACKER:

☐ ....
☐ ....
☐ ....
☐ ....
☐ ....

8am: ....
9am: ....
10am: ....
11am: ....
12pm: ....
1pm: ....
2pm: ....
3pm: ....
4pm: ....
5pm: ....
6pm: ....
7pm: ....
8pm: ....
9pm: ....
10pm: ....

"Rowing harder doesn't help if the boat is headed in the wrong direction."

KENICHI OHMAE

End of day check-in

WHAT WENT WELL TODAY?

HOW CAN I IMPROVE TOMORROW?

THREE THINGS I AM GRATEFUL FOR TODAY

TODAY I'VE FELT...

Friday

DATE:

TOP 3 PRIORITIES:

1. ....
....
....

2. ....
....
....

3. ....
....
....

HABIT TRACKER:

☐ ....
☐ ....
☐ ....
☐ ....
☐ ....

DAILY INTENTION:

8am: ....
9am: ....
10am: ....
11am: ....
12pm: ....
1pm: ....
2pm: ....
3pm: ....
4pm: ....
5pm: ....
6pm: ....
7pm: ....
8pm: ....
9pm: ....
10pm: ....

" Real change, enduring change, happens one step at a time."

RUTH BADER GINSBURG

End of day check-in

WHAT WENT WELL TODAY?

HOW CAN I IMPROVE TOMORROW?

THREE THINGS I AM GRATEFUL FOR TODAY

TODAY I'VE FELT...

Weekend

DATE:

WEEKEND INTENTION:

TOP 3 PRIORITIES:

1. ....

   ....

   ....

2. ....

   ....

   ....

3. ....

   ....

   ....

HABIT TRACKER:

- ☐ ....
- ☐ ....
- ☐ ....
- ☐ ....
- ☐ ....

9am: ....

10am: ....

11am: ....

12pm: ....

1pm: ....

2pm: ....

3pm: ....

4pm: ....

5pm: ....

6pm: ....

7pm: ....

8pm: ....

9pm: ....

10pm: ....

"Just one small positive thought in the morning can change your whole day."

DALAI LAMA XIV

Weekend

DATE:

3 THINGS I AM GRATEFUL FOR THIS WEEKEND:

1. ....
....
....

2. ....
....
....

3. ....
....
....

9am: ....
10am: ....
11am: ....
12pm: ....
1pm: ....
2pm: ....
3pm: ....
4pm: ....
5pm: ....
6pm: ....
7pm: ....
8pm: ....
9pm: ....
10pm: ....

HABIT TRACKER:

☐ ....
☐ ....
☐ ....
☐ ....
☐ ....

THIS WEEKEND I'VE FELT...

End of week check-in

WHAT WERE MY INTENTIONS THIS WEEK?

HOW DID I FOCUS ON MY INTENTIONS THIS WEEK?

WHAT ELSE DID I LEARN?

> *" If you don't like something, change it.*
> *If you can't change it, change your attitude."*
>
> MAYA ANGELOU

WHAT WERE MY TOP 5 ACHIEVEMENTS THIS WEEK?

WHAT THINGS MADE ME HAPPY THIS WEEK?

HOW WILL I MAKE NEXT WEEK AMAZING?

Week Two
Change Your Habits

What habits will help you achieve your goals and intentions? The next part of this journey is picking and sticking to the good habits that are right for you.

Picking and Sticking to Good Habits

Now that we have our goals and intentions in place, it's time to think about what habits we need to be able to achieve them. You may have already noticed the habit tracker on your daily pages - and perhaps even started using it. This week, we're going to really hone in to what habits are needed to make your goals and intentions a reality, how to start slow and build your way up, and what to do if you fall off the wagon. By ensuring we focus on the right habits, and build them up slowly, we can stay on the right track to achieving whatever it is we want to achieve by the end of these 12 weeks.

WHAT HABITS DO YOU REALLY WANT TO FOCUS ON?

Before you start putting a whole load of new habits on your tracker, in the hopes that they'll help you achieve your goals and intentions, I want you to spend some time really thinking about which habits are going to help you move forward.

To do this, I'd like you to think back on those goals and intentions from last week and write a list of at least 10 habits you think you need in your life to be able to achieve them. Perhaps you wanted to bring more balance into your life, so a daily meditation practice could be one of your new habits. Maybe you think drinking more water or moving your body every day would help you achieve your goal. Whatever they are, scribble down at least 10 on a scrap piece of paper (or on the My Brain Dump page)!

Once you've got them all down, I want you to go back and pick what you think is the most important habit off that list. Which one will make the biggest difference in your life? Which one gets you excited? Head to your Week 2 planner section and pop that one in the top spot.

Now, go back through this list and pick four more in order of priority. You should end up with the five habits that you believe will help you achieve the goals and intentions you set in Week 1. Make sure they're habits that make you feel excited and will make the biggest difference to your life and well-being.

SMALL STEPS LEAD TO BIG STEPS

When we start something new, it's easy to think that we'll wake up the next morning and be a completely different person. We'll tell ourselves that tomorrow we'll drink more water, exercise every day, eat well, meditate, and so on. However, we can often put too much on our plates and begin to get overwhelmed with all of these changes in our life.

So, with your newly chosen habits, I'd like you to pick just the top one from your list to focus on this week and next. In Week 4, you can add your second habit to the habit tracker – but only if you're ready. Every two weeks, or whenever you're ready, add another of your chosen habits to the habit tracker.

The key is to start slow and focus on one habit at a time, building on these as you go. Only when you feel as though you have the previous habit down should you then move onto the next. If that takes you longer than these 12 weeks, then that is more than okay! Don't feel pressured to add a new habit to your daily routine until you are fully ready.

WHAT TO DO IF YOU FALL OFF THE WAGON

I am going to be totally honest with you here: we all fall off the wagon. There are going to be days when things don't go to plan and you can't make time for that particular habit today. The key to success is not never missing a day on your habit tracker. Success comes when you have the right tools in place to get back on the wagon, without letting a fear of failure take over.

If you instantly think, 'Great, I've missed one day of exercise, there's no point in carrying on', then you've undone all of your hard work for one momentary blip. In the resources for Week 2, alongside a guide to picking and sticking to habits, I have a video explaining my favourite analogy: the ice cube analogy. This is a great illustration of why you should never throw in the towel after a bad day or even a bad week.

Finally, in your planner for Week 2, there's a section to fill in some positive habit affirmations. I have included a resource online for you to pick some of your favourites, but you could also come up with your own! Whenever you feel as though you may be ready to 'give it all up', come back to this section and repeat these affirmations to yourself. These can help change your inner monologue from 'I'm a failure, what's the point?' to something far more productive that can help keep you going.

ONLINE RESOURCES FOR WEEK 2

* Article: An in-depth guide to picking and sticking to habits

* Article: Positive habit affirmations

* Video: Bex explains the ice cube analogy for when you fall off the wagon

www.theantiburnoutclub.com/journal

Week Two: Change Your Habits

Make a list of at least 10 habits on a scrap piece of paper or on the My Brain Dump page, before picking your top five to focus on.

1. ....

2. ....

3. ....

4. ....

5. ....

Here is a space for your favourite positive habit affirmations (see Week 2 online resources).

....

....

....

....

....

....

....

....

....

....

....

Remember, if you feel as though you're slipping off the wagon, come back and repeat these affirmations to yourself.

WEEK COMMENCING:

ONE BIG GOAL FOR THE WEEK:

THIS WEEK WILL BE AMAZING IF I ALSO ACHIEVE...

IMPORTANT THINGS TO REMEMBER THIS WEEK:

Monday:

1. ....

Tuesday:

....

2. ....

Wednesday:

....

3. ....

Thursday:

....

Friday:

4. ....

Saturday:

....

5. ....

Sunday:

....

NOTES FOR THIS WEEK:

Monday

DATE:

DAILY INTENTION:

TOP 3 PRIORITIES:

1. ....
....
....

2. ....
....
....

3. ....
....
....

HABIT TRACKER:

☐ ....
☐ ....
☐ ....
☐ ....
☐ ....

8am: ....
9am: ....
10am: ....
11am: ....
12pm: ....
1pm: ....
2pm: ....
3pm: ....
4pm: ....
5pm: ....
6pm: ....
7pm: ....
8pm: ....
9pm: ....
10pm: ....

"First forget inspiration. Habit is more dependable. Habit will sustain you whether you're inspired or not."

OCTAVIA E. BUTLER

End of day check-in

WHAT WENT WELL TODAY?

HOW CAN I IMPROVE TOMORROW?

THREE THINGS I AM GRATEFUL FOR TODAY

TODAY I'VE FELT...

Tuesday

DATE:

TOP 3 PRIORITIES:

1. ....
....

....

....

2. ....

....

....

3. ....

....

....

HABIT TRACKER:

☐ ....

☐ ....

☐ ....

☐ ....

☐ ....

8am: ....

9am: ....

10am: ....

11am: ....

12pm: ....

1pm: ....

2pm: ....

3pm: ....

4pm: ....

5pm: ....

6pm: ....

7pm: ....

8pm: ....

9pm: ....

10pm: ....

*" Every action you take is a
vote for the type of person
you wish to become."*

JAMES CLEAR

WEEK TWO | 38

End of day check-in

WHAT WENT WELL TODAY?

HOW CAN I IMPROVE TOMORROW?

THREE THINGS I AM GRATEFUL FOR TODAY

TODAY I'VE FELT...

Wednesday

DATE:

DAILY INTENTION:

TOP 3 PRIORITIES:

1. ....
....
....

2. ....
....
....

3. ....
....
....

HABIT TRACKER:

☐ ....

☐ ....

☐ ....

☐ ....

☐ ....

8am: ....

9am: ....

10am: ....

11am: ....

12pm: ....

1pm: ....

2pm: ....

3pm: ....

4pm: ....

5pm: ....

6pm: ....

7pm: ....

8pm: ....

9pm: ....

10pm: ....

"If you believe you can change - if you make it a habit - the change becomes real."

CHARLES DUHIGG

End of day check-in

WHAT WENT WELL TODAY?

HOW CAN I IMPROVE TOMORROW?

THREE THINGS I AM GRATEFUL FOR TODAY

TODAY I'VE FELT...

Thursday

DATE:

TOP 3 PRIORITIES:

1. ....

....

....

2. ....

....

....

3. ....

....

....

HABIT TRACKER:

☐ ....

☐ ....

☐ ....

☐ ....

☐ ....

DAILY INTENTION:

8am: ....

9am: ....

10am: ....

11am: ....

12pm: ....

1pm: ....

2pm: ....

3pm: ....

4pm: ....

5pm: ....

6pm: ....

7pm: ....

8pm: ....

9pm: ....

10pm: ....

"Good habits are worth being fanatical about."

JOHN IRVING

End of day check-in

WHAT WENT WELL TODAY?

HOW CAN I IMPROVE TOMORROW?

THREE THINGS I AM GRATEFUL FOR TODAY

TODAY I'VE FELT...

Friday

DATE:

DAILY INTENTION:

TOP 3 PRIORITIES:

1. ....
....
....

2. ....
....
....

3. ....
....
....

HABIT TRACKER:

☐ ....
☐ ....
☐ ....
☐ ....
☐ ....

8am: ....
9am: ....
10am: ....
11am: ....
12pm: ....
1pm: ....
2pm: ....
3pm: ....
4pm: ....
5pm: ....
6pm: ....
7pm: ....
8pm: ....
9pm: ....
10pm: ....

"Drop by drop is the water pot filled."

BUDDHA

End of day check-in

WHAT WENT WELL TODAY?

HOW CAN I IMPROVE TOMORROW?

THREE THINGS I AM GRATEFUL FOR TODAY

TODAY I'VE FELT...

Weekend

DATE:

WEEKEND INTENTION:

TOP 3 PRIORITIES:

1. ....

....

....

2. ....

....

....

3. ....

....

....

9am: ....

10am: ....

11am: ....

12pm: ....

1pm: ....

2pm: ....

3pm: ....

4pm: ....

5pm: ....

6pm: ....

7pm: ....

8pm: ....

9pm: ....

10pm: ....

HABIT TRACKER:

☐ ....

☐ ....

☐ ....

☐ ....

☐ ....

"Happiness is a habit - cultivate it."

ELBERT HUBBARD

Weekend

DATE:

3 THINGS I AM GRATEFUL FOR THIS WEEKEND:

1.

2.

3.

9am:

10am;

11am:

12pm:

1pm:

2pm:

3pm:

4pm:

5pm:

6pm:

7pm:

8pm:

9pm:

10pm;

HABIT TRACKER:

☐
☐
☐
☐
☐

THIS WEEKEND I'VE FELT...

WEEK TWO: CHANGE YOUR HABITS
End of week check-in

WHICH HABITS DID I PICK TO FOCUS ON FIRST?

WHAT WILL I DO IF I MISS A DAY OR TWO OF MY NEW HABITS?

WHAT ELSE DID I LEARN?

"Practice isn't the thing you do once you're good. It's the thing you do that makes you good."

MALCOLM GLADWELL

WHAT WERE MY TOP 5 ACHIEVEMENTS THIS WEEK?

WHAT THINGS MADE ME HAPPY THIS WEEK?

HOW WILL I MAKE NEXT WEEK AMAZING?

Week Three
Be Grateful

Why is practising daily gratitude so good for us? It turns out, gratitudes don't just make for pretty Instagram pictures... there's a real science behind the power of gratitude too!

Practising Daily Gratitude

You will have already noticed the section in each daily planner that gives you the space to write down three gratitudes and perhaps you've already started using it. However, this week, I want us to dig deep into why practising gratitude is so important, how we can focus on our gratitude each day, and when the best time to do this is. Once we understand the importance of daily gratitude, it will (hopefully) become one of your most helpful habits going forward.

THE PROVEN BENEFITS OF GRATITUDE

There are plenty of scientific studies about the benefits of gratitude with some astonishing results. In one of my favourite TED Talks of all time (The Happy Secret to Better Work), positive psychology author Shawn Achor conducted a study into whether gratitude could actually rewire our minds to think differently. What this study found was that those who wrote down three things they're grateful for each day, for 21 days, started automatically looking for the good in each day. Their brains stopped scanning the world for negative news, which we see so much of sometimes, and instead actively sought out the positive.

More research by psychologist Robert Emmons, from the University of California, Davis, found that simply keeping a gratitude journal could significantly increase well-being and life satisfaction once it became a habit. This research also identified a whole range of physical, psychological and social benefits to practising gratitude daily.

It goes even further than that, too. In a clinical study published in the *American Psychologist* journal, researchers found that after just one thoughtful gratitude practice, participants were 10% happier and saw a 35% reduction in depressive symptoms.

In your online resources for this week, I have included some of the many interesting research papers on the topic of gratitude and the TED Talk by Shawn Achor, for those who want to dig a little deeper.

HOW TO PRACTISE GRATITUDE

So now we know why gratitude is so good for us, what's the best way to practise it? Well, I think there's no time like the present! Before you even finish this lesson today, I'd like you to head to your Week 3 planner section and write down three things that you're grateful for right now. After all, we know that even just the one-time act of gratitude can boost our happiness!

Done that? Amazing work! If you did struggle to come up with three things that you're grateful for, however, then know that you're not alone. If we've spent a long time focusing on the negative, then it can be tough to rewire our brains in the beginning. Regular practise, however, can help this become second nature.

You can practise gratitude in a multitude of ways, depending on what works for you. However, here are some of my own top tips:

* **Get specific:** In the beginning, we may be quite vague with our gratitudes ('I'm grateful for my dog, my family, my friends'). However, to really expand on this try getting a bit more specific each day. For example, 'I'm grateful that my friend called me today because she knew I had an important meeting'. This helps us look outside of the more obvious gratitudes. Dig deep!

* **Turn it into a game:** Struggling to find anything to be grateful for? Turn it into a game! Challenge yourself to find a positive in everything, no matter how small or silly. You can also reframe situations that may initially seem negative into something more positive in this way. For example, 'My friend cancelled on me today, but I'm grateful that it meant I didn't need to get dressed'.

* **Extend your gratitude to someone else:** If you've put a particular person on your gratitude list, have you told them? If not, why not? Let your friend know you're grateful they called! I'll expand more on this in Week 7, too.

ADDING GRATITUDE TO YOUR EVENING ROUTINE

We now know the benefits of practising gratitude and how to do it, but to really ensure this works for you then you need to make it a habit! There is a section in your daily planner to write down three gratitudes every weekday evening and three for each weekend. When you do this before you go to sleep, your brain is thinking about all of the positives for that day instead of focusing on the negatives. You may find it easier to drift off to sleep knowing that, whatever happened, there is some good in each day.

To ensure you turn this into a habit, I'd like you to set a reminder on your phone for the same time each evening. When will you complete your end of day check-in and those three gratitudes? Fill in the pledge in your Week 3 planner with that time to make yourself the promise that you'll stick to this new, positive habit.

ONLINE RESOURCES FOR WEEK 3

* Video: How gratitude journalling changed my life with Bex

* Article: Dig deep into the power of gratitude, more resources on the studies and research

www.theantiburnoutclub.com/journal

Week Three: Be Grateful

Write down three things that you are grateful for right now!

1. ....

2. ....

3. ....

Now you know the benefits of gratitude, commit to a daily practice by filling in the pledge below.

I .... (name) commit to practising gratitude every evening. I will set aside time in my evening routine at .... (time) to write down between one and three things I am grateful for that day. I know that focusing on gratitude for the day can help me feel more positive and empowered, and see the good in every day.

Signed: Date:

....

Remember, practising gratitude is only a couple of minutes of your time each day but can have such a huge impact on your well-being. Keep going!

WEEK COMMENCING:

ONE BIG GOAL FOR THE WEEK:

THIS WEEK WILL BE AMAZING IF I ALSO ACHIEVE...

1. ....
   ....

2. ....
   ....

3. ....
   ....

4. ....
   ....

5. ....
   ....

IMPORTANT THINGS TO REMEMBER THIS WEEK:

Monday:

Tuesday:

Wednesday:

Thursday:

Friday:

Saturday:

Sunday:

NOTES FOR THIS WEEK:

Monday

DATE:

DAILY INTENTION:

TOP 3 PRIORITIES:

1. ....

....

....

2. ....

....

....

3. ....

....

....

HABIT TRACKER:

☐ ....
☐ ....
☐ ....
☐ ....
☐ ....

8am: ....
9am: ....
10am: ....
11am: ....
12pm: ....
1pm: ....
2pm: ....
3pm: ....
4pm: ....
5pm: ....
6pm: ....
7pm: ....
8pm: ....
9pm: ....
10pm: ....

"The more you praise and celebrate your life, the more there is in life to celebrate."

OPRAH WINFREY

End of day check-in

WHAT WENT WELL TODAY?

HOW CAN I IMPROVE TOMORROW?

THREE THINGS I AM GRATEFUL FOR TODAY

TODAY I'VE FELT...

Tuesday

DATE:

DAILY INTENTION:

TOP 3 PRIORITIES:

1. ....
....
....

2. ....
....
....

3. ....
....
....

HABIT TRACKER:

☐ ....
☐ ....
☐ ....
☐ ....
☐ ....

8am: ....
9am: ....
10am: ....
11am: ....
12pm: ....
1pm: ....
2pm: ....
3pm: ....
4pm: ....
5pm: ....
6pm: ....
7pm: ....
8pm: ....
9pm: ....
10pm: ....

*"Gratitude is a divine emotion:
it fills the heart, but not to bursting;
it warms it, but not to fever."*

CHARLOTTE BRONTË

End of day check-in

WHAT WENT WELL TODAY?

HOW CAN I IMPROVE TOMORROW?

THREE THINGS I AM GRATEFUL FOR TODAY

TODAY I'VE FELT...

Wednesday

DATE:

DAILY INTENTION:

TOP 3 PRIORITIES:

1. ....
....
....

2. ....
....
....

3. ....
....
....

HABIT TRACKER:

☐ ....
☐ ....
☐ ....
☐ ....
☐ ....

8am: ....
9am: ....
10am: ....
11am: ....
12pm: ....
1pm: ....
2pm: ....
3pm: ....
4pm: ....
5pm: ....
6pm: ....
7pm: ....
8pm: ....
9pm: ....
10pm: ....

"Wear gratitude like a cloak, and it will feed every corner of your life."

RUMI

End of day check-in

WHAT WENT WELL TODAY?

HOW CAN I IMPROVE TOMORROW?

THREE THINGS I AM GRATEFUL FOR TODAY

TODAY I'VE FELT...

Thursday

DATE:

TOP 3 PRIORITIES:

1. ....
....
....

2. ....
....
....

3. ....
....
....

HABIT TRACKER:

☐ ....
☐ ....
☐ ....
☐ ....
☐ ....

DAILY INTENTION:

8am: ....
9am: ....
10am: ....
11am: ....
12pm: ....
1pm: ....
2pm: ....
3pm: ....
4pm: ....
5pm: ....
6pm: ....
7pm: ....
8pm: ....
9pm: ....
10pm: ....

"Gratitude makes sense of our past, brings peace for today, and creates a vision for tomorrow."

MELODY BEATTIE

End of day check-in

WHAT WENT WELL TODAY?

HOW CAN I IMPROVE TOMORROW?

THREE THINGS I AM GRATEFUL FOR TODAY

TODAY I'VE FELT...

Friday

DATE:

DAILY INTENTION:

TOP 3 PRIORITIES:

1. ....

   ....

   ....

2. ....

   ....

   ....

3. ....

   ....

   ....

HABIT TRACKER:

- ☐ ....
- ☐ ....
- ☐ ....
- ☐ ....
- ☐ ....

8am: ....

9am: ....

10am: ....

11am: ....

12pm: ....

1pm: ....

2pm: ....

3pm: ....

4pm: ....

5pm: ....

6pm: ....

7pm: ....

8pm: ....

9pm: ....

10pm: ....

"Gratitude turns what we have into enough."

MELODY BEATTIE

End of day check-in

WHAT WENT WELL TODAY?

HOW CAN I IMPROVE TOMORROW?

THREE THINGS I AM GRATEFUL FOR TODAY

TODAY I'VE FELT...

Weekend

DATE:

WEEKEND INTENTION:

TOP 3 PRIORITIES:

1. ....
....
....

2. ....
....
....

3. ....
....
....

9am: ....
10am: ....
11am: ....
12pm: ....
1pm: ....
2pm: ....
3pm: ....
4pm: ....
5pm: ....
6pm: ....
7pm: ....
8pm: ....
9pm: ....
10pm: ....

HABIT TRACKER:

☐ ....
☐ ....
☐ ....
☐ ....
☐ ....

" Piglet noticed that even though he had a Very Small Heart, it could hold a rather large amount of Gratitude."

A.A. MILNE

Weekend

DATE: _____

3 THINGS I AM GRATEFUL FOR THIS WEEKEND:

1. ....

....

....

2. ....

....

....

3. ....

....

....

9am: ....
10am: ....
11am: ....
12pm: ....
1pm: ....
2pm: ....
3pm: ....
4pm: ....
5pm: ....
6pm: ....
7pm: ....
8pm: ....
9pm: ....
10pm: ....

HABIT TRACKER:

☐ ....
☐ ....
☐ ....
☐ ....
☐ ....

THIS WEEKEND I'VE FELT...

End of week check-in

HOW HAS PRACTISING DAILY GRATITUDE FELT THIS WEEK?

HOW WILL I MAKE SURE I STICK AT THIS NEW POSITIVE HABIT?

WHAT ELSE DID I LEARN?

> *"Once you begin to take note of the things you are grateful for, you begin to lose sight of the things that you lack."*

GERMANY KENT

WHAT WERE MY TOP 5 ACHIEVEMENTS THIS WEEK?

WHAT THINGS MADE ME HAPPY THIS WEEK?

HOW WILL I MAKE NEXT WEEK AMAZING?

Week Four
Move Your Body

Movement can make us feel amazing, but when we're feeling stressed or unhappy it seems almost impossible to find the motivation. This week is all about getting you moving.

Moving Your Body

You probably already know the physical benefits of moving your body on a regular basis, but did you know that movement can help reduce stress and increase happiness too? The difficulty is, when we're feeling stressed or unhappy, we rarely want to exercise. It's a tough cycle to break, but I'm hoping that I can help with some motivational tricks to get you moving. We've done this challenge time and time again at The Anti-Burnout Club and the results are always astounding. So, if you want to move more but struggle to do so every day, then this one is for you. And if you are naturally motivated to exercise, then perhaps this will add some fun into the mix too.

JUST ONE SONG

When you think about moving your body, how does it make you feel? Perhaps you don't feel very motivated to move right now. Maybe you know it will make you feel better, but you can't find the energy to get changed into workout gear or trainers and get moving. You may even feel motivated to move, but you're just not sure you can face another HIIT workout or run around the block.

If this is the case, I want you to try this challenge for me. I'd like you to pick just one song that makes you feel happy and energised and then move for the duration of that one song. That's it. It doesn't matter what kind of exercise you do, as long as you're moving for the whole song. You could walk to the end of the road and back, do star jumps on the spot, or (a personal favourite) treat yourself to a kitchen disco. If you do have any kind of mobility issues then you can move in your seat – this technique is suitable for everyone!

Once the song is over, decide what you want to do next. Do you want to take it up a level and move to another song? If so, keep going! If not, that's okay. You still moved for a few minutes longer than you would have done before. There is plenty of time to expand on this technique and get moving for longer when you feel the time is right.

THE 2-MINUTE TRICK

The 'just one song' approach is a variation of my 2-minute trick, which I've included in this week's online resources. Most of us will have the motivation to do something for just a couple of minutes. Telling ourselves we'll work out for an hour can often have the reverse effect on our motivation levels. We just can't bring ourselves to do it. However, just a couple of minutes is fine!

You may find that once you've got the ball rolling and the blood is pumping through your body, you'll want to carry on through a few songs. You might even end up doing the full hour before you know it!

You can use this trick for pretty much anything that you're feeling unmotivated for; whether it's moving your body, cleaning the house or working on an important project. Promise yourself that you'll move, clean or work for just one song. And then see how you feel after.

MAKE IT A DAILY HABIT

We're now in Week 4, which means it's time to add another positive habit to your habit tracker, if you feel ready to do so. Perhaps you've already added a habit to do with exercise or moving your body, and you'll use this trick to get motivated. If not, consider making this your daily habit to focus on for the next two weeks.

Daily movement has so many benefits, from reducing your risk of heart disease through to boosting mental health and improving sleep. Promising yourself that you'll move for just one song every day isn't a huge, unachievable goal, but it's one that can really improve your quality of life.

TAKING IT FURTHER

Once you've got into the habit of moving for just one song, hopefully daily, then you can expand on this technique further. During this challenge at The Anti-Burnout Club, we usually make a group playlist packed full of energising and uplifting songs. I have included a couple of these in the online resources for this week.

If you want to take your movement further, then try making a playlist full of songs that make you want to move. That way, if your 'one song' is over and you feel motivated to keep going, you will be able to immediately without searching for another song and getting out of the groove.

Finally, create your own movement plan using the Week 4 planner to decide how you want to move and to choose some songs to get moving to. That way, if you feel motivation waning, you've already done a lot of the hard work. Just pick a song and a movement, and get to it!

ONLINE RESOURCES FOR WEEK 4

✳ Video: The 2-minute trick explained with Bex

✳ A couple of our group-made playlists to help you move your body more

www.theantiburnoutclub.com/journal

Week Four: Move Your Body

Write down your favourite songs to move to.

....

....

....

....

....

....

....

Write down your favourite ways of moving (e.g. walking, running, dancing, yoga, etc.).

....

....

....

....

....

....

....

This is your movement plan! If you ever feel unmotivated, come back to this to pick a song and a way to move for the duration of that song!

WEEK COMMENCING:	ONE BIG GOAL FOR THE WEEK:

THIS WEEK WILL BE AMAZING IF I ALSO ACHIEVE...

IMPORTANT THINGS TO REMEMBER THIS WEEK:

1. ....

Monday:

....

Tuesday:

2. ....

Wednesday:

....

Thursday:

3. ....

....

Friday:

4. ....

Saturday:

....

5. ....

Sunday:

....

NOTES FOR THIS WEEK:

Monday

DATE:

DAILY INTENTION:

TOP 3 PRIORITIES:

1. ....
....
....

2. ....
....
....

3. ....
....
....

HABIT TRACKER:

☐ ....
☐ ....
☐ ....
☐ ....
☐ ....

8am: ....
9am: ....
10am: ....
11am: ....
12pm: ....
1pm: ....
2pm: ....
3pm: ....
4pm: ....
5pm: ....
6pm: ....
7pm: ....
8pm: ....
9pm: ....
10pm: ....

"Exercise is a celebration of what your body can do. Not a punishment for what you ate."

KEVIN NG

End of day check-in

WHAT WENT WELL TODAY?

HOW CAN I IMPROVE TOMORROW?

THREE THINGS I AM GRATEFUL FOR TODAY

TODAY I'VE FELT...

Tuesday

DAILY INTENTION:
_____

DATE:

TOP 3 PRIORITIES:

1. ....
....
....

2. ....
....
....

3. ....
....
....

HABIT TRACKER:

☐ ....
☐ ....
☐ ....
☐ ....
☐ ....

8am: ....
9am: ....
10am: ....
11am: ....
12pm: ....
1pm: ....
2pm: ....
3pm: ....
4pm: ....
5pm: ....
6pm: ....
7pm: ....
8pm: ....
9pm: ....
10pm: ....

" Exercise is a keystone habit that triggers widespread change."

CHARLES DUHIGG

End of day check-in

WHAT WENT WELL TODAY?

HOW CAN I IMPROVE TOMORROW?

THREE THINGS I AM GRATEFUL FOR TODAY

TODAY I'VE FELT...

Wednesday

DATE:

DAILY INTENTION:

TOP 3 PRIORITIES:

1. ....
   ....
   ....

2. ....
   ....
   ....

3. ....
   ....
   ....

HABIT TRACKER:

☐ ....
☐ ....
☐ ....
☐ ....
☐ ....

8am: ....
9am: ....
10am: ....
11am: ....
12pm: ....
1pm: ....
2pm: ....
3pm: ....
4pm: ....
5pm: ....
6pm: ....
7pm: ....
8pm: ....
9pm: ....
10pm: ....

"If you don't make time for exercise, you'll probably have to make time for illness."

ROBIN SHARMA

End of day check-in

WHAT WENT WELL TODAY?

HOW CAN I IMPROVE TOMORROW?

THREE THINGS I AM GRATEFUL FOR TODAY

TODAY I'VE FELT...

Thursday

DATE:

DAILY INTENTION:

TOP 3 PRIORITIES:

1. ....

....

....

2. ....

....

....

3. ....

....

....

HABIT TRACKER:

☐ ....

☐ ....

☐ ....

☐ ....

☐ ....

8am: ....

9am: ....

10am: ....

11am: ....

12pm: ....

1pm: ....

2pm: ....

3pm: ....

4pm: ....

5pm: ....

6pm: ....

7pm: ....

8pm: ....

9pm: ....

10pm: ....

" If you are in a bad mood go for
a walk. If you are still in a bad
mood go for another walk."

HIPPOCRATES

End of day check-in

WHAT WENT WELL TODAY?

HOW CAN I IMPROVE TOMORROW?

THREE THINGS I AM GRATEFUL FOR TODAY

TODAY I'VE FELT...

Friday

DAILY INTENTION:

DATE:

TOP 3 PRIORITIES:

1.

2.

3.

HABIT TRACKER:

☐
☐
☐
☐
☐

8am:
9am:
10am:
11am:
12pm:
1pm:
2pm:
3pm:
4pm:
5pm:
6pm:
7pm:
8pm:
9pm:
10pm:

"Take care of your body. It's the only place you have to live in."

JIM ROHN

End of day check-in

WHAT WENT WELL TODAY?

HOW CAN I IMPROVE TOMORROW?

THREE THINGS I AM GRATEFUL FOR TODAY

TODAY I'VE FELT...

Weekend

DATE:

WEEKEND INTENTION:

TOP 3 PRIORITIES:

1. ....

....

....

2. ....

....

....

3. ....

....

....

HABIT TRACKER:

☐ ....

☐ ....

☐ ....

☐ ....

☐ ....

9am: ....

10am: ....

11am: ....

12pm: ....

1pm: ....

2pm: ....

3pm: ....

4pm: ....

5pm: ....

6pm: ....

7pm: ....

8pm: ....

9pm: ....

10pm: ....

" All that is important is this one moment in movement. Make the moment important, vital, and worth living."

MARTHA GRAHAM

Weekend

DATE:

3 THINGS I AM GRATEFUL FOR THIS WEEKEND:

1. ....

....

....

2. ....

....

....

3. ....

....

....

9am: ....

10am: ....

11am: ....

12pm: ....

1pm: ....

2pm: ....

3pm: ....

4pm: ....

5pm: ....

6pm: ....

7pm: ....

8pm: ....

9pm: ....

10pm: ....

HABIT TRACKER:

☐ ....

☐ ....

☐ ....

☐ ....

☐ ....

THIS WEEKEND I'VE FELT...

WEEK FOUR: MOVE YOUR BODY

End of week check-in

WHAT MOVEMENT DID I GET IN THIS WEEK?

HOW DOES MOVING MY BODY MAKE ME FEEL?

WHAT ELSE DID I LEARN?

> "When it comes to health and well-being, regular exercise is about as close to a magic potion as you can get."

THICH NHAT HANH

WHAT WERE MY TOP 5 ACHIEVEMENTS THIS WEEK?

WHAT THINGS MADE ME HAPPY THIS WEEK?

HOW WILL I MAKE NEXT WEEK AMAZING?

Week Five
Become Mindful

You don't need to spend hours locked in a dark room to be mindful. Mindfulness can be practised anywhere and at practically any time. This week, we'll learn how to do just that.

Mindful Moments

Whenever I talk to people about mindfulness, I get a lot of eye rolls and a 'How am I supposed to fit that into my day?!' questions. You might be thinking the same right now. However, I want to show you that mindful moments don't need time or for you to shut yourself away. In fact, mindfulness can be done at any time, anywhere, and even while you're doing other things. There's a common misconception that mindfulness is meditation and while we do have a whole week dedicated to the wonders of meditation, Week 5 is all about how we can fit more mindful moments in - without having to dedicate time to specifically practising meditation.

WHAT EXACTLY IS MINDFULNESS?

So, if mindfulness isn't the same as meditation, what exactly is it? To quote the modern master of mindfulness, Jon Kabat-Zinn: 'Mindfulness is awareness, cultivated by paying attention in a sustained and particular way: on purpose, in the present moment, and non-judgmentally'.

Basically, mindfulness is the ability to be fully present. We're aware of all that is around us, without judging, reacting or becoming overwhelmed by it. Meditation can certainly help develop mindfulness, but you don't need to meditate to be mindful!

Mindful techniques are also often used in different types of therapy, including cognitive behaviour therapy (CBT) and dialectical behaviour therapy (DBT) in order to help patients better understand their thoughts, feelings and emotions without judgement.

THE IMPORTANCE OF MINDFUL MOMENTS

When we live mindlessly (that is, the opposite of mindfully) it can become easy to get swept away by all that is going on around us. We may often feel stressed, overcome with emotion, and perhaps even overwhelmed.

By spending time being present and mindful, we can reduce stress, cut out ruminating and unhelpful thoughts, become less reactive, improve focus, and so much more. There are also countless studies that have looked into the physical benefits of becoming more mindful, including reducing blood pressure and even improving digestion!

Mindfulness allows us to step back and see the bigger picture. It can bring clarity to situations that seem overwhelming or impossible to cope with. It can stop those ruminating thoughts that can make us feel low or anxious. From personal experience, mindfulness really can change your life – and you don't need to spend hours a day meditating to reap the benefits.

HOW TO FIT MORE MINDFUL MOMENTS INTO YOUR DAY

While there are plenty of ways to practise being more mindful, such as yoga, meditation, and even tai chi, you don't always need to set time aside for mindfulness. In fact, I try to squeeze mindful moments into as many different parts of my day as I can, including:

* When brushing my teeth

* Making a cup of tea

* Showering

* Washing the dishes

* On trains/buses

* Eating

* Time I'd normally scroll on my phone

You see, mindfulness is just about being present – and that means you can do it whenever you'd normally be on autopilot. Those times when your mind just drifts off, usually worrying about all of the things you have to do that day... That is when you want to be mindful!

Simply bringing your awareness to what you're doing, any thoughts or feelings, and any sensations or senses is the act of being mindful. Whether that's water running over your body in the shower or the scenery whizzing past you on the train.

In your resources this week, you'll find a quick mindful moment that you can pop your headphones on and enjoy, even if you're doing the washing up.

5-4-3-2-1 TECHNIQUE

If you need a brief mindfulness activity for when you're feeling anxious or overwhelmed, try this technique:

5. Bring your attention to and acknowledge 5 things you can see.

4. Bring your attention to and acknowledge 4 things you can touch.

3. Bring your attention to and acknowledge 3 things you can hear.

2. Bring your attention to and acknowledge 2 things you can smell.

1. Bring your attention to and acknowledge 1 thing you can taste.

Along with a quick mindful moment video in your online resources for this week, you'll also find a longer introduction to mindfulness and some top book recommendations for further reading.

Mindfulness is a skill that can take time to master, but it's one of the most valuable skills I have ever learnt. Enjoy!

ONLINE RESOURCES FOR WEEK 5

* Video: A longer introduction to mindfulness and its benefits with Bex

* Video: A quick mindful moment with Bex

* Article: Top book recommendations to learn more about mindfulness

www.theantiburnoutclub.com/journal

Week Five: Become Mindful

When can I practise being more mindful during the day? (Pick a few of your usual daily activities to slot mindfulness into.)

....

....

....

....

....

Use the space below to keep track of any mindful moments during this week (and beyond).

Date/Time	What was I doing?/ How was I feeling?	How do I feel now?

Being more mindful can help you ditch the sense of being overwhelmed and the rumination – and it slots into most daily activities!

WEEK COMMENCING:

ONE BIG GOAL FOR THE WEEK:

THIS WEEK WILL BE AMAZING IF I ALSO ACHIEVE...

1. ....
....

2. ....
....

3. ....
....

4. ....
....

5. ....
....

IMPORTANT THINGS TO REMEMBER THIS WEEK:

Monday:

Tuesday:

Wednesday:

Thursday:

Friday:

Saturday:

Sunday:

NOTES FOR THIS WEEK:

Monday

DATE:

DAILY INTENTION:

TOP 3 PRIORITIES:

1. ....

....

....

2. ....

....

....

3. ....

....

....

HABIT TRACKER:

☐ ....

☐ ....

☐ ....

☐ ....

☐ ....

8am: ....

9am: ....

10am: ....

11am: ....

12pm: ....

1pm: ....

2pm: ....

3pm: ....

4pm: ....

5pm: ....

6pm: ....

7pm: ....

8pm: ....

9pm: ....

10pm: ....

"The little things? The little moments? They aren't little."

JON KABAT-ZINN

End of day check-in

WHAT WENT WELL TODAY?

HOW CAN I IMPROVE TOMORROW?

THREE THINGS I AM GRATEFUL FOR TODAY

TODAY I'VE FELT...

Tuesday

DATE:

DAILY INTENTION:

TOP 3 PRIORITIES:

1. ....
   ....
   ....
2. ....
   ....
   ....
3. ....
   ....
   ....

HABIT TRACKER:

☐ ....
☐ ....
☐ ....
☐ ....
☐ ....

8am: ....
9am: ....
10am; ....
11am: ....
12pm: ....
1pm: ....
2pm: ....
3pm: ....
4pm: ....
5pm: ....
6pm: ....
7pm: ....
8pm: ....
9pm: ....
10pm; ....

" Live the actual moment.
Only this actual moment is life."

THICH NHAT HANH

End of day check-in

WHAT WENT WELL TODAY?

HOW CAN I IMPROVE TOMORROW?

THREE THINGS I AM GRATEFUL FOR TODAY

TODAY I'VE FELT...

Wednesday

DATE:

TOP 3 PRIORITIES:

1. ....

....

....

2. ....

....

....

3. ....

....

....

WEEK FIVE | 100

HABIT TRACKER:

☐ ....

☐ ....

☐ ....

☐ ....

☐ ....

8am: ....

9am: ....

10am: ....

11am: ....

12pm: ....

1pm: ....

2pm: ....

3pm: ....

4pm: ....

5pm: ....

6pm: ....

7pm: ....

8pm: ....

9pm: ....

10pm: ....

"You are the sky. Everything else is just the weather."

PEMA CHÖDRÖN

End of day check-in

WHAT WENT WELL TODAY?

HOW CAN I IMPROVE TOMORROW?

THREE THINGS I AM GRATEFUL FOR TODAY

TODAY I'VE FELT...

Thursday

DATE:

DAILY INTENTION:

TOP 3 PRIORITIES:

1. ....

....

....

2. ....

....

....

3. ....

....

....

HABIT TRACKER:

☐ ....

☐ ....

☐ ....

☐ ....

☐ ....

8am: ....

9am: ....

10am: ....

11am: ....

12pm: ....

1pm: ....

2pm: ....

3pm: ....

4pm: ....

5pm: ....

6pm: ....

7pm: ....

8pm: ....

9pm: ....

10pm: ....

"What would it be like if I could accept life - accept this moment exactly as it is?"

TARA BRACH

End of day check-in

WHAT WENT WELL TODAY?

HOW CAN I IMPROVE TOMORROW?

THREE THINGS I AM GRATEFUL FOR TODAY

TODAY I'VE FELT...

Friday

DATE:

DAILY INTENTION:

TOP 3 PRIORITIES:

1. ....
....
....

2. ....
....
....

3. ....
....
....

8am: ....
9am: ....
10am: ....
11am: ....
12pm: ....
1pm: ....
2pm: ....
3pm: ....
4pm: ....
5pm: ....
6pm: ....
7pm: ....
8pm: ....
9pm: ....
10pm: ....

HABIT TRACKER:

☐ ....
☐ ....
☐ ....
☐ ....
☐ ....

"Our life is shaped by our mind,
for we become what we think."

BUDDHA

End of day check-in

WHAT WENT WELL TODAY?

HOW CAN I IMPROVE TOMORROW?

THREE THINGS I AM GRATEFUL FOR TODAY

TODAY I'VE FELT...

Weekend

DATE:

TOP 3 PRIORITIES:

1. ....

....

....

2. ....

....

....

3. ....

....

....

HABIT TRACKER:

☐ ....

☐ ....

☐ ....

☐ ....

☐ ....

9am: ....

10am: ....

11am: ....

12pm: ....

1pm: ....

2pm: ....

3pm: ....

4pm: ....

5pm: ....

6pm: ....

7pm: ....

8pm: ....

9pm: ....

10pm: ....

" Mindfulness isn't difficult,
we just need to remember to do it."

SHARON SALZBERG

Weekend

DATE: _____

3 THINGS I AM GRATEFUL
FOR THIS WEEKEND:

1. ....
....
....

2. ....
....
....

3. ....
....
....

9am: ....
10am; ....
11am: ....
12pm: ....
1pm: ....
2pm: ....
3pm: ....
4pm: ....
5pm: ....
6pm: ....
7pm: ....
8pm: ....
9pm: ....
10pm; ....

HABIT TRACKER:

☐ ....
☐ ....
☐ ....
☐ ....
☐ ....

THIS WEEKEND I'VE FELT...

End of week check-in

WHERE DID I MANAGE TO SQUEEZE IN MINDFUL MOMENTS THIS WEEK?

HOW DID BEING MORE MINDFUL MAKE ME FEEL?

WHAT ELSE DID I LEARN?

> "When we get too caught up in the busyness of the world, we lose connection with one another - and ourselves."

JACK KORNFIELD

WHAT WERE MY TOP 5 ACHIEVEMENTS THIS WEEK?

WHAT THINGS MADE ME HAPPY THIS WEEK?

HOW WILL I MAKE NEXT WEEK AMAZING?

Week Six
Unplug Yourself

It can feel worrying how much time we spend on our phones or with other technology, and it certainly doesn't help with burnout. This week we're going to slowly, but surely, unplug.

The Joys of Unplugging

Now, I truly believe that technology has its benefits: bringing people together, easier access to information, and even enabling the expansion of this journal with online resources. However, there are also plenty of downsides that come with being glued to our phones, tablets and laptops every day. This week, I want us to spend some time thinking about our reliance on technology - however daunting that may seem! We're then going to gradually add in some times during our days when we can 'unplug' and break free from the constant scrolling we've become so accustomed to.

HOW MUCH TIME DO YOU SPEND ON YOUR PHONE?

The average person is believed to pick up their phone between 60 and 100 times every day. Often, we do this without even thinking. How many times have you found yourself scrolling and don't even remember what you picked your phone up for in the first place?

The most recent studies into how long people spend on their phone puts the average person at between 3-4 hours a day. Multiply that by seven days and you have around 24 hours per week - one whole day! It's quite scary when you look at that figure and think about what else you could do with that time, but I don't want you to chastise yourself and swear off your phone forever.

To start, I would simply like you to check in on your phone usage. Most smartphones are now designed with apps to show you how much time you spend on them, so check-in and see what your average is per day or per week. Don't look at this with judgement, just acknowledge that this is how much time you spend on your phone. You can pop that number in your Week 6 planner to start.

GRADUALLY REDUCING TECH TIME

Now you know how long you spend on your phone, you can start trying to gradually reduce that time. Like I said, it's important you don't try to cut everything out at once (think about those small steps from the Change Your Habits week). Going cold turkey isn't going to be beneficial and will likely cause anxiety or stress that you don't need. So, commit to a number of minutes you want to reduce your phone time by, that you think is doable. My advice would be to start by reducing it by 15 minutes this week and then slowly build on that; 30 minutes less next week, 45 minutes less the week after, and so on.

There's a space in your weekly planner to jot down how many minutes you're going to reduce your phone usage by each week, and to keep track of how things are going.

ANXIOUS ABOUT UNPLUGGING?

The thought of unplugging, even for just a little while, may seem quite daunting. After all, technology companies are very good at trying to keep our attention and making sure our focus is always on our phone. If you're feeling anxious about unplugging, know that this is completely normal.

The important thing to remember is that you are going to take it slowly. You may find that as you start to reduce your phone time, it becomes easier to go longer without it. Technology has become a modern-day addiction and that means weaning ourselves off it is a process. Use the quick unplugging tips below to make life a little easier.

QUICK UNPLUGGING TIPS

Not sure when to unplug? Or how to? Here are my top tips for reducing your phone or technology usage:

* **Before bed:** Hands up if you probably use your phone most when you're trying to drift off to sleep? Start by reducing your phone usage before bed to see the most benefits. Not only will it help you fall asleep, but it might even save you money... Most of us do the majority of our online shopping when we're in bed!

* **When you wake up:** If you use your phone before falling asleep, then it's likely to be the first thing you reach for in the morning too. Try investing in a proper alarm clock so that you can put your phone out of the way and can't pick it up first thing in the morning.

* **Use apps:** It may seem counterintuitive to use technology to beat our technology addictions, but there are plenty of helpful apps that can help you put down the phone. You'll find a list of my favourites in this week's online resources.

There are countless benefits to getting less screen time, which I've covered in the online resources. So, even if it feels scary, let's try putting our phones down... even for just a little bit.

ONLINE RESOURCES FOR WEEK 6

* Article: Even more top tips for unplugging

* Video: The real mental health benefits of unplugging

* Article: Top apps that can help you reduce phone usage

www.theantiburnoutclub.com/journal

Week Six: Unplug Yourself

How much time do I spend on my phone currently?

....

How many minutes do I want to reduce this by each week?

....

Keep track of your unplugging progress here.

Week	Total time	Reduced by (mins)	Notes

Take it step by step and don't panic if you fall off the wagon one week! Just go back to your goal for the week before and keep unplugging.

WEEK COMMENCING: _____

ONE BIG GOAL FOR THE WEEK: _____

THIS WEEK WILL BE AMAZING IF I ALSO ACHIEVE...

1. ....
   ....

2. ....
   ....

3. ....
   ....

4. ....
   ....

5. ....
   ....

IMPORTANT THINGS TO REMEMBER THIS WEEK:

Monday:

Tuesday:

Wednesday:

Thursday:

Friday:

Saturday:

Sunday:

NOTES FOR THIS WEEK:

Monday

DATE:

DAILY INTENTION:

TOP 3 PRIORITIES:

1. ....

....

....

2. ....

....

....

3. ....

....

....

HABIT TRACKER:

☐ ....

☐ ....

☐ ....

☐ ....

☐ ....

8am: ....

9am: ....

10am: ....

11am: ....

12pm: ....

1pm: ....

2pm: ....

3pm: ....

4pm: ....

5pm: ....

6pm: ....

7pm: ....

8pm: ....

9pm: ....

10pm: ....

"The more ways we have to connect, the more many of us seem desperate to unplug."

PICO IYER

End of day check-in

WHAT WENT WELL TODAY?

HOW CAN I IMPROVE TOMORROW?

THREE THINGS I AM GRATEFUL FOR TODAY

TODAY I'VE FELT...

Tuesday

DATE:

TOP 3 PRIORITIES:

1. ....
....
....

2. ....
....
....

3. ....
....
....

HABIT TRACKER:

☐ ....

☐ ....

☐ ....

☐ ....

☐ ....

DAILY INTENTION:

8am: ....

9am: ....

10am: ....

11am: ....

12pm: ....

1pm: ....

2pm: ....

3pm: ....

4pm: ....

5pm: ....

6pm: ....

7pm: ....

8pm: ....

9pm: ....

10pm: ....

"Especially when you have a lot going on, you must find a way to unplug and focus on yourself."

MANDY INGBER

End of day check-in

WHAT WENT WELL TODAY?

HOW CAN I IMPROVE TOMORROW?

THREE THINGS I AM GRATEFUL FOR TODAY

TODAY I'VE FELT...

Wednesday

DATE:

DAILY INTENTION:
_____

TOP 3 PRIORITIES:

1. ....
....
....

2. ....
....
....

3. ....
....
....

HABIT TRACKER:

☐ ....
☐ ....
☐ ....
☐ ....
☐ ....

8am: ....
9am: ....
10am: ....
11am: ....
12pm: ....
1pm: ....
2pm: ....
3pm: ....
4pm: ....
5pm: ....
6pm: ....
7pm: ....
8pm: ....
9pm: ....
10pm: ....

"Being connected to everything has disconnected us from ourselves and the preciousness of this present moment."

L.M. BROWNING

End of day check-in

WHAT WENT WELL TODAY?

HOW CAN I IMPROVE TOMORROW?

THREE THINGS I AM GRATEFUL FOR TODAY

TODAY I'VE FELT...

Thursday

DATE:

DAILY INTENTION:

TOP 3 PRIORITIES:

1. ....
....
....

2. ....
....
....

3. ....
....
....

HABIT TRACKER:

☐ ....
☐ ....
☐ ....
☐ ....
☐ ....

8am: ....
9am: ....
10am: ....
11am: ....
12pm: ....
1pm: ....
2pm: ....
3pm: ....
4pm: ....
5pm: ....
6pm: ....
7pm: ....
8pm: ....
9pm: ....
10pm: ....

"Almost everything will work again if you unplug it for a few minutes... including yourself."

ANNE LAMOTT

End of day check-in

WHAT WENT WELL TODAY?

HOW CAN I IMPROVE TOMORROW?

THREE THINGS I AM GRATEFUL FOR TODAY

TODAY I'VE FELT...

Friday

DATE:

TOP 3 PRIORITIES:

1. ....

....

....

2. ....

....

....

3. ....

....

....

HABIT TRACKER:

☐ ....

☐ ....

☐ ....

☐ ....

☐ ....

DAILY INTENTION:

8am: ....

9am: ....

10am: ....

11am: ....

12pm: ....

1pm: ....

2pm: ....

3pm: ....

4pm: ....

5pm: ....

6pm: ....

7pm: ....

8pm: ....

9pm: ....

10pm: ....

"Unplugging gives you the chance to remember who you are at your core."

ARIN MURPHY-HISCOCK

End of day check-in

WHAT WENT WELL TODAY?

HOW CAN I IMPROVE TOMORROW?

THREE THINGS I AM GRATEFUL FOR TODAY

TODAY I'VE FELT...

Weekend

DATE:

WEEKEND INTENTION:

TOP 3 PRIORITIES:

1. ....
   ....
   ....

2. ....
   ....
   ....

3. ....
   ....
   ....

HABIT TRACKER:

☐ ....
☐ ....
☐ ....
☐ ....
☐ ....

9am: ....
10am: ....
11am: ....
12pm: ....
1pm: ....
2pm: ....
3pm: ....
4pm: ....
5pm: ....
6pm: ....
7pm: ....
8pm: ....
9pm: ....
10pm: ....

"If we can't unplug from that machine, eventually we're going to become mindless."

ALAN LIGHTMAN

Weekend

DATE: _____

3 THINGS I AM GRATEFUL FOR THIS WEEKEND:

1. _____

_____

_____

2. _____

_____

_____

3. _____

_____

_____

9am: _____

10am: _____

11am: _____

12pm: _____

1pm: _____

2pm: _____

3pm: _____

4pm: _____

5pm: _____

6pm: _____

7pm: _____

8pm: _____

9pm: _____

10pm: _____

HABIT TRACKER:

☐ _____

☐ _____

☐ _____

☐ _____

☐ _____

THIS WEEKEND I'VE FELT...

End of week check-in

HOW DID REDUCING MY PHONE USAGE GO THIS WEEK?

WHAT TECHNIQUES WILL I USE TO HELP ME REDUCE THIS MORE?

WHAT ELSE DID I LEARN?

> "We have to disconnect from all our omnipresent devices - our gadgets, our screens, our social media - and reconnect with ourselves."

ARIANNA HUFFINGTON

WHAT WERE MY TOP 5 ACHIEVEMENTS THIS WEEK?

WHAT THINGS MADE ME HAPPY THIS WEEK?

HOW WILL I MAKE NEXT WEEK AMAZING?

Week Seven
Be Kind

Did you know that Random Acts of Kindness don't just make the recipient feel good? Being kind can boost our happy hormones too! This week we're going to spread happiness wherever we go.

Exploring Random Acts of Kindness

It's kind to be kind! However, did you know that little Random Acts of Kindness (RAOK) can do so much for our mental health? This week, we're going to focus on bringing some light into other people's days – and improving our own well-being at the same time. I'll cover some of the proven benefits of doing things for others, give you a few acts of kindness to try out, and ensure we're not giving too much of ourselves away in the meantime. This is a fun week with some mood-boosting benefits that you'll want to keep coming back to time and time again.

THE BENEFITS OF RANDOM ACTS OF KINDNESS

Doing something nice for someone else has one very obvious benefit: making someone else's day. However, there are plenty of scientifically proven benefits that indicate that Random Acts of Kindness can actually do so much for our own well-being too.

The Random Acts of Kindness Foundation (that's a real thing!) have published countless studies that show the benefits of kindness include:

* Producing oxytocin, the 'love hormone'. This can help reduce blood pressure and improve overall self-esteem.

* Producing serotonin, which can regulate your mood, help you feel calmer, and even improve memory.

* Producing endorphins, which can reduce pain and boost your mood.

* Experiencing the 'helper's high', which is when your brain's pleasure and reward centres light up after being kind to someone.

* Reducing cortisol (the stress hormone) levels and even reducing anxiety symptoms.

These are just some of the many, many benefits of being kind, and I've included all of the research in this week's online resources.

SMALL RANDOM ACTS OF KINDNESS TO TRY

So, where do we start with bringing more kindness into our days? If you watched the Shawn Achor TED Talk I reference in our Be Grateful week, then you may have noticed he also discusses small acts of kindness every day. In his study, he encouraged people to reach out to a colleague and send them an email thanking them for something – however small.

This is the perfect way to start with your Random Acts of Kindness: reaching out to people and thanking them. It doesn't need to be an email to a colleague, of course. You can get in touch with anyone in your life that you want to say thank you to. Tell them how grateful you are for them, how much you care for them, what you love about them, and anything you think might bring a smile to their face.

Once you've got into the swing of things with this, you can then expand your Random Acts of Kindness into other areas. Perhaps telling a stranger you love their outfit, stopping to ask the shop assistant if they're having a nice day, and so on. In the online resources, I have included seven little Random Acts of Kindness challenges you can try to tick off this week, so see how you get on.

Finally, you can move on to much greater acts of kindness such as volunteering for a cause you care about. However, there is one important thing to remember as you embark on this journey of kindness...

DON'T CONFUSE RAOK WITH PEOPLE-PLEASING

If you are prone to burning out, then this is an important piece of advice for you this week. We can often feel as though being kind to others must come before being kind to ourselves, which then leads to people-pleasing. Perhaps we think we need to say 'Yes' to everything to be kind to other people. Trust me, this is a one-way ticket to burnout!

So, as you're going through this week, ensure that you're compassionate to yourself too. Please don't say yes to something just because you think that's the kind thing to do. Putting yourself first is the kindest thing you can do for anyone. As they say, you can't pour from an empty cup.

To finish off this week's online resources, I have included a mindful moment for self-compassion. If you're prone to people-pleasing, saying yes, or putting others before yourself, then I'd really recommend spending a few minutes with that mindful moment.

Don't be afraid to set boundaries and say 'No' if someone is asking too much from you!

This week is definitely a fun one and I'd love to know how you get on, and how these Random Acts of Kindness make you feel. Fill in your Week 7 planner with the thoughts, feelings and emotions after each act of kindness and use this to come back to whenever you need a boost of happy hormones.

ONLINE RESOURCES FOR WEEK 7

* Article: Proven benefits of Random Acts of Kindness

* Video: Seven little Random Acts of Kindness to try this week!

* Video: Mindful moment for self-compassion

www.theantiburnoutclub.com/journal

Week Seven: Be Kind

Who am I going to be kind to this week and how?

....

....

....

....

....

....

....

....

How did the Random Acts of Kindness make me feel?

....

....

....

....

....

Remember to start small and don't overpromise or people-please!
Little messages of thanks are a great way to get started this week.

WEEK COMMENCING:

ONE BIG GOAL FOR THE WEEK:

THIS WEEK WILL BE AMAZING IF I ALSO ACHIEVE...

IMPORTANT THINGS TO REMEMBER THIS WEEK:

Monday:

1. ....
....

Tuesday:

2. ....
....

Wednesday:

3. ....
....

Thursday:

Friday:

4. ....
....

Saturday:

5. ....
....

Sunday:

NOTES FOR THIS WEEK:

Monday

DATE:

DAILY INTENTION:

TOP 3 PRIORITIES:

1. ....
   ....
   ....

2. ....
   ....
   ....

3. ....
   ....
   ....

HABIT TRACKER:

☐ ....
☐ ....
☐ ....
☐ ....
☐ ....

8am: ....
9am: ....
10am: ....
11am: ....
12pm: ....
1pm: ....
2pm: ....
3pm: ....
4pm: ....
5pm: ....
6pm: ....
7pm: ....
8pm: ....
9pm: ....
10pm: ....

*"I think probably kindness
is my number one attribute
in a human being."*

ROALD DAHL

End of day check-in

WHAT WENT WELL TODAY?

HOW CAN I IMPROVE TOMORROW?

THREE THINGS I AM GRATEFUL FOR TODAY

TODAY I'VE FELT...

Tuesday

DATE:

DAILY INTENTION:

TOP 3 PRIORITIES:

1. ....
....
....

2. ....
....
....

3. ....
....
....

HABIT TRACKER:

☐ ....
☐ ....
☐ ....
☐ ....
☐ ....

8am: ....
9am: ....
10am: ....
11am: ....
12pm: ....
1pm: ....
2pm: ....
3pm: ....
4pm: ....
5pm: ....
6pm: ....
7pm: ....
8pm: ....
9pm: ....
10pm: ....

"Kindness can become its own motive.
We are made kind by being kind."

ERIC HOFFER

End of day check-in

WHAT WENT WELL TODAY?

HOW CAN I IMPROVE TOMORROW?

THREE THINGS I AM GRATEFUL FOR TODAY

TODAY I'VE FELT...

Wednesday

DATE:

TOP 3 PRIORITIES:

1. ....
....
....

2. ....
....
....

3. ....
....
....

HABIT TRACKER:

☐ ....
☐ ....
☐ ....
☐ ....
☐ ....

DAILY INTENTION:

8am: ....
9am: ....
10am: ....
11am: ....
12pm: ....
1pm: ....
2pm: ....
3pm: ....
4pm: ....
5pm: ....
6pm: ....
7pm: ....
8pm: ....
9pm: ....
10pm: ....

"Be kind whenever possible.
It is always possible."

DALAI LAMA XIV

End of day check-in

WHAT WENT WELL TODAY?

HOW CAN I IMPROVE TOMORROW?

THREE THINGS I AM GRATEFUL FOR TODAY

TODAY I'VE FELT...

Thursday

DATE:

TOP 3 PRIORITIES:

1. ....
   ....
   ....

2. ....
   ....
   ....

3. ....
   ....
   ....

HABIT TRACKER:

☐ ....
☐ ....
☐ ....
☐ ....
☐ ....

DAILY INTENTION:

8am: ....
9am: ....
10am: ....
11am: ....
12pm: ....
1pm: ....
2pm: ....
3pm: ....
4pm: ....
5pm: ....
6pm: ....
7pm: ....
8pm: ....
9pm: ....
10pm: ....

" Practise random kindness and
senseless acts of beauty."

ANNE HERBERT

End of day check-in

WHAT WENT WELL TODAY?

HOW CAN I IMPROVE TOMORROW?

THREE THINGS I AM GRATEFUL FOR TODAY

TODAY I'VE FELT...

Friday

DATE:

DAILY INTENTION:

TOP 3 PRIORITIES:

1. ....
   ....
   ....

2. ....
   ....
   ....

3. ....
   ....
   ....

8am: ....
9am: ....
10am: ....
11am: ....
12pm: ....
1pm: ....
2pm: ....
3pm: ....
4pm: ....
5pm: ....
6pm: ....
7pm: ....
8pm: ....
9pm: ....
10pm: ....

HABIT TRACKER:

☐ ....
☐ ....
☐ ....
☐ ....
☐ ....

"What wisdom can you find that is greater than kindness?"

JEAN-JACQUES ROUSSEAU

End of day check-in

WHAT WENT WELL TODAY?

HOW CAN I IMPROVE TOMORROW?

THREE THINGS I AM GRATEFUL FOR TODAY

TODAY I'VE FELT...

Weekend

DATE:

TOP 3 PRIORITIES:

1. ....
....
....

2. ....
....
....

3. ....
....
....

HABIT TRACKER:

☐ ....
☐ ....
☐ ....
☐ ....
☐ ....

WEEKEND INTENTION:

9am: ....
10am: ....
11am: ....
12pm: ....
1pm: ....
2pm: ....
3pm: ....
4pm: ....
5pm: ....
6pm: ....
7pm: ....
8pm: ....
9pm: ....
10pm: ....

"Remember there's no such thing as
a small act of kindness. Every act
creates a ripple with no logical end."

SCOTT ADAMS

Weekend

DATE:

3 THINGS I AM GRATEFUL FOR THIS WEEKEND:

1. ....
   ....
   ....

2. ....
   ....
   ....

3. ....
   ....
   ....

9am: ....

10am: ....

11am: ....

12pm: ....

1pm: ....

2pm: ....

3pm: ....

4pm: ....

5pm: ....

6pm: ....

7pm: ....

8pm: ....

9pm: ....

10pm: ....

HABIT TRACKER:

☐ ....

☐ ....

☐ ....

☐ ....

☐ ....

THIS WEEKEND I'VE FELT...

☺ ☐ ☐ ☐ ☐ ☐ ☹

End of week check-in

WHAT RANDOM ACT(S) OF KINDNESS DID I DO THIS WEEK?

HOW WILL I EXPAND ON THESE RAOKS?

WHAT ELSE DID I LEARN?

> *"Carry out a random act of kindness, with no expectation of reward, safe in the knowledge that one day someone might do the same for you."*
>
> PRINCESS DIANA

WHAT WERE MY TOP 5 ACHIEVEMENTS THIS WEEK?

WHAT THINGS MADE ME HAPPY THIS WEEK?

HOW WILL I MAKE NEXT WEEK AMAZING?

Week Eight
Try Meditation

One of the most effective ways to become more mindful is through meditation, and this week I've roped in one of the best of the best to show you how.

Getting More Mindful with Meditation

As I mentioned during our Become Mindful week, meditation is an amazing way to become more mindful. When it comes to stress, burnout and feeling overwhelmed, there are few remedies as powerful as regular meditation. But if you're new to it all, then it can seem daunting. Luckily, this week I've roped in the help of the incredible Kristy Lomas, founder of The Ki Retreat. Kristy has over 15 years' experience as a multi-disciplined therapist, including meditation, reiki and other forms of holistic well-being and healing.

THE PROOF THAT MEDITATION IS GOOD FOR US

While many cultures have spoken about the benefits of meditation for thousands of years, it's only really in the last two decades that researchers have studied just how powerful it can be – and there's still so much to learn! There have been studies into the long-term impact of regular meditation, that show how it can improve our resilience to stress, increase our compassion, reduce the signs and symptoms of some mental health conditions, and even have a positive impact on our physical health!

Just like we discussed in Week 5, when talking about mindfulness, meditation can improve lots of different aspects of our lives. So as not to bog you down in all of the science at once, I have included another online resource this week that brings together all of the best bits of the studies around meditation and mindfulness. When you have time, take a look through and make a note of what you want to get out of regular meditating.

SOME TIPS AND TRICKS TO GET THE MOST OUT OF MEDITATING

If you're new to meditation or just trying to ensure you're getting the most out of your practice, here are some top tips and tricks to help:

* **Gradually increase over time:** Studies have shown that meditation is most effective when we practise it regularly. However, not all of us can commit to 20-30 minutes (or more) of meditation every day. Start with just a few minutes a few times a week, before building up. It's the best way to make meditation a healthy habit!

* **Don't try too hard:** One of the biggest difficulties people face is that they try too hard to switch off or relax. It actually feels quite counterintuitive not to try, but this is exactly how meditation works. If you find yourself 'trying' to relax, perhaps leave the meditation for the time being and come back to it at a later date.

* **Always get comfortable:** While you may see pictures of people meditating cross-legged, if that's not comfortable for you then don't do it! The last thing you want is your focus to be on how uncomfortable you feel. Sit down, lie down, grab a blanket, whatever feels comfy.

* **It can take time, don't give up:** Meditation is a skill just like any other. It can take time to hone that skill and your brain needs the practice to understand what's being asked of it. Just like you wouldn't expect to run a marathon with 10 minutes of training, don't expect meditation to be a simple 'one lesson and I'm a pro' kind of vibe. Keep coming back to it, keep learning and growing, and it will come in time.

* **Some days will be easier than others:** Whether you've just started meditating or you've been doing it for years, there will always be days when it's easier to do than others. The key is not to beat yourself up if you struggle one day. Don't force it, just come back when you're ready.

* **This is your journey:** Both Kristy and I could give you a ton of our own advice to 'help you meditate' but just know that this is your journey, your experience. If you like meditating at night in bed, then do that. If you like going outside and meditating first thing in the morning, then do that. If you like meditating once a week or twice a day, then do that. This is your time, make it work for you.

Meditation is such a powerful way to become more mindful and I really hope you enjoy bringing some of that into your days. It's a brilliant way to beat the burnout, so enjoy the experience of being kind to your mind!

ONLINE RESOURCES FOR WEEK 8

* Video: An introduction to meditation with Kristy Lomas

* Video: A 20-minute meditation session with Kristy Lomas

* Article: The studies that show how good meditation is for us

www.theantiburnoutclub.com/journal

Week Eight: Try Meditation

What does meditating mean to you? Are you brand new to it or is it something you already love?

....

....

....

....

....

....

Use this space to jot down any thoughts, feelings and/or emotions straight after meditating.

....

....

....

....

....

....

At the end of the week we'll see how you found the meditation lesson and if it's something you can see yourself doing more often. So, consider this as you go through the week.

WEEK COMMENCING:

ONE BIG GOAL FOR THE WEEK:

THIS WEEK WILL BE AMAZING IF I ALSO ACHIEVE...

1. ....

....

2. ....

....

3. ....

....

4. ....

....

5. ....

....

IMPORTANT THINGS TO REMEMBER THIS WEEK:

Monday:

Tuesday:

Wednesday:

Thursday:

Friday:

Saturday:

Sunday:

NOTES FOR THIS WEEK:

Monday

DATE:

DAILY INTENTION:

TOP 3 PRIORITIES:

1. ....
....
....

2. ....
....
....

3. ....
....
....

HABIT TRACKER:

☐ ....
☐ ....
☐ ....
☐ ....
☐ ....

8am: ....
9am: ....
10am: ....
11am: ....
12pm: ....
1pm: ....
2pm: ....
3pm: ....
4pm: ....
5pm: ....
6pm: ....
7pm: ....
8pm: ....
9pm: ....
10pm: ....

" Your goal is not to battle with the mind, but to witness the mind."

SWAMI MUKTANANDA

End of day check-in

WHAT WENT WELL TODAY?

HOW CAN I IMPROVE TOMORROW?

THREE THINGS I AM GRATEFUL FOR TODAY

TODAY I'VE FELT...

Tuesday

DATE:

TOP 3 PRIORITIES:

1. ....
....
....

2. ....
....
....

3. ....
....
....

HABIT TRACKER:

- ☐ ....
- ☐ ....
- ☐ ....
- ☐ ....
- ☐ ....

DAILY INTENTION:

8am: ....
9am: ....
10am: ....
11am: ....
12pm: ....
1pm: ....
2pm: ....
3pm: ....
4pm: ....
5pm: ....
6pm: ....
7pm: ....
8pm: ....
9pm: ....
10pm: ....

"Calmness of mind is one of the beautiful jewels of wisdom."

JAMES ALLEN

End of day check-in

WHAT WENT WELL TODAY?

HOW CAN I IMPROVE TOMORROW?

THREE THINGS I AM GRATEFUL FOR TODAY

TODAY I'VE FELT...

Wednesday

DATE:

DAILY INTENTION:

TOP 3 PRIORITIES:

1. ....

   ....

   ....

2. ....

   ....

   ....

3. ....

   ....

   ....

HABIT TRACKER:

☐ ....

☐ ....

☐ ....

☐ ....

☐ ....

8am: ....

9am: ....

10am: ....

11am: ....

12pm: ....

1pm: ....

2pm: ....

3pm: ....

4pm: ....

5pm: ....

6pm: ....

7pm: ....

8pm: ....

9pm: ....

10pm: ....

"I have lived with several Zen masters - all of them cats."

ECKHART TOLLE

End of day check-in

WHAT WENT WELL TODAY?

HOW CAN I IMPROVE TOMORROW?

THREE THINGS I AM GRATEFUL FOR TODAY

TODAY I'VE FELT...

Thursday

DATE:

TOP 3 PRIORITIES:

1. ....
   ....
   ....

2. ....
   ....
   ....

3. ....
   ....
   ....

HABIT TRACKER:

☐ ....
☐ ....
☐ ....
☐ ....
☐ ....

DAILY INTENTION:

8am: ....
9am: ....
10am: ....
11am: ....
12pm: ....
1pm: ....
2pm: ....
3pm: ....
4pm: ....
5pm: ....
6pm: ....
7pm: ....
8pm: ....
9pm: ....
10pm: ....

"The best meditation is effortless. The best meditation is a gentle awareness."

MAXIME LAGACÉ

End of day check-in

WHAT WENT WELL TODAY?

HOW CAN I IMPROVE TOMORROW?

THREE THINGS I AM GRATEFUL FOR TODAY

TODAY I'VE FELT...

Friday

DATE:

TOP 3 PRIORITIES:

1. ....

....

....

2. ....

....

....

3. ....

....

....

HABIT TRACKER:

☐ ....

☐ ....

☐ ....

☐ ....

☐ ....

DAILY INTENTION:

8am: ....

9am: ....

10am: ....

11am: ....

12pm: ....

1pm: ....

2pm: ....

3pm: ....

4pm: ....

5pm: ....

6pm: ....

7pm: ....

8pm: ....

9pm: ....

10pm: ....

" Meditation is like a gym in which you develop the powerful mental muscles of calm and insight."

AJAHN BRAHM

End of day check-in

WHAT WENT WELL TODAY?

HOW CAN I IMPROVE TOMORROW?

THREE THINGS I AM GRATEFUL FOR TODAY

TODAY I'VE FELT...

Weekend

DATE:

WEEKEND INTENTION:

TOP 3 PRIORITIES:

1. ....
....
....

2. ....
....
....

3. ....
....
....

HABIT TRACKER:

☐ ....
☐ ....
☐ ....
☐ ....
☐ ....

9am: ....
10am: ....
11am: ....
12pm: ....
1pm: ....
2pm: ....
3pm: ....
4pm: ....
5pm: ....
6pm: ....
7pm: ....
8pm: ....
9pm: ....
10pm: ....

"When meditation is mastered, the mind is unwavering like the flame of a candle in a windless place."

THE BHAGAVAD GITA

Weekend

DATE:

3 THINGS I AM GRATEFUL FOR THIS WEEKEND:

1. ....
....
....

2. ....
....
....

3. ....
....
....

9am: ....
10am: ....
11am: ....
12pm: ....
1pm: ....
2pm: ....
3pm: ....
4pm: ....
5pm: ....
6pm: ....
7pm: ....
8pm: ....
9pm: ....
10pm: ....

HABIT TRACKER:

☐ ....
☐ ....
☐ ....
☐ ....
☐ ....

THIS WEEKEND I'VE FELT...

WEEK EIGHT: TRY MEDITATION
End of week check-in

HOW WAS THE MEDITATION LESSON FOR ME THIS WEEK?

IS THIS SOMETHING I CAN SEE MYSELF DOING OFTEN? HOW AND WHEN?

WHAT ELSE DID I LEARN?

"The more regularly and the more deeply you meditate, the sooner you will find yourself acting always from a centre of peace."

J. DONALD WALTERS

WHAT WERE MY TOP 5 ACHIEVEMENTS THIS WEEK?

WHAT THINGS MADE ME HAPPY THIS WEEK?

HOW WILL I MAKE NEXT WEEK AMAZING?

Week Nine
Fuel Your Body and Mind

Fuelling my body and mind in the right way has had one of the biggest impacts on my stress and energy levels, and my overall mood. This week, the nutritionists and I are talking about all things food!

Fuelling Your Body and Mind

What we put into our bodies can have a direct impact on the structure and function of our brains, and ultimately, therefore, our mood. You may have noticed feeling a bit tired or grumpy after a night of highly processed and sugary food – and that's because we haven't given our brains and bodies the right fuel to feel good. It's incredible how much of a difference fuelling our bodies in the right way can have on our energy levels, stress levels, and even our happiness.

In this section, we're going to look at why what we eat is so important, how to eat to feel amazing, how to take it step-by-step, and even cover some quick and easy feel-good recipes on the site. What is key, however, is that this is all about fuelling your body and not about dieting. If you fuel your body in the right way, this will have a positive impact on all aspects of your health – physically and mentally – and that's what we want to achieve!

WHY WHAT WE EAT IS SO IMPORTANT

Imagine your body is a top of the range car. When it gets low on energy, it needs refuelling to get it working again. When you eat sugary and/ or processed foods, you're putting in low-quality fuel that might get the car moving, but not at the standard you'd expect from a high-performance vehicle! However, when you eat food that is packed full of vitamins and minerals, you're putting the very best fuel into your body. This then nourishes your brain and ensures that the high-performance vehicle (your body) works to the very best of its abilities.

As mentioned, what we eat can also have a big impact on stress and energy levels, and even our happy hormones. However, it's a two-way street! Feeling stressed and anxious can also wreak havoc with our digestive system and cause issues such as IBS. So, making sure we're always keeping our bodies and brains fuelled effectively can play such a big part in our health overall.

EATING TO FEEL GOOD

This week, I want us to focus on eating to feel good as opposed to anything else. Before you reach for the delivery apps, stop and think; ask yourself, 'Will this just make me feel rubbish tomorrow?'. Chances are if the food is beige and processed, it will! So, start by making small changes to the way you fuel your body and make a note of any differences you feel in your mood and energy levels.

With this lesson, you will find two really useful videos from our nutritionists, Anna and Emily. In the first, Anna sets you a challenge to eat 30 plant-based foods in a week. Don't worry if that sounds like a lot – you'd be surprised at what counts as a plant-based food (bread is in)! The key here is to improve your gut health with a variety of different fruits, vegetables, nuts, seeds and grains – all of which can do wonders for your mental health too.

In the second video, Emily has some excellent tips for beating the afternoon slump and eating to improve your energy levels. I'll let you into a little secret: apparently crisps and chocolate aren't the best choices (who knew?!).

Also, we have put together seven easy recipes that will help you eat to feel good. Each should take less than 20 minutes to prepare and won't need any fancy ingredients. The aim is to get you in the kitchen to see how quick it can be to put together delicious and nutritious food.

FIND NUTRITION OVERWHELMING?

I know that nutrition can seem overwhelming; as someone who has tried every diet, had issues with emotional eating, and spent way too much on processed food in my life, I am still learning how to fuel my body the right way. However, this week is designed as a little taster of what could be such a positive lifestyle change for you. So, as always, start slow and record any changes in your mind and well-being.

Don't go from eating three takeaways a week to cutting out all sugar and processed foods! You'll likely feel worse rather than better if you attempt such drastic changes in the beginning.

So:

* If you can't hit 30 plant-based foods this week, try improving by five a week. If you hit 30 this week, try 35 the week after.

* If you can only find time to do one of the recipes this week, that's fine. Try another one the week after and so on.

* If you struggle to give up the crisps or chocolate, look for smarter alternatives and swap one out each week.

Most importantly, enjoy your food! Sit down at the table with loved ones, savour every mouthful, and spend time being more mindful with the cooking and eating process. I promise you, these small changes will have a huge impact in themselves.

ONLINE RESOURCES FOR WEEK 9

* Article: Seven quick, easy recipes to fuel your body

* Video: Tips to beat the afternoon slump and eat for energy with nutritionist Emily

* Video: 30 plant-based foods challenge with nutritionist Anna

www.theantiburnoutclub.com/journal

Week Nine: Fuel Your Body and Mind

Use this space to write down what you usually eat in a week and what you think this does for your energy and stress levels.

....

....

....

....

....

....

Once you have watched Anna's 30 plant-based foods challenge, use this space to keep track of your 30.

....

....

....

....

....

....

Don't forget to check out the free recipes in this week's online resources for inspiration!

WEEK COMMENCING:	ONE BIG GOAL FOR THE WEEK:

THIS WEEK WILL BE AMAZING IF I ALSO ACHIEVE...	IMPORTANT THINGS TO REMEMBER THIS WEEK:
	Monday:
1.	
	Tuesday:
2.	
	Wednesday:
	Thursday:
3.	
	Friday:
4.	
	Saturday:
5.	Sunday:

NOTES FOR THIS WEEK:

Monday

DATE:

DAILY INTENTION:

TOP 3 PRIORITIES:

1. ....
....
....

2. ....
....
....

3. ....
....
....

HABIT TRACKER:

☐ ....
☐ ....
☐ ....
☐ ....
☐ ....

8am: ....
9am: ....
10am: ....
11am: ....
12pm: ....
1pm: ....
2pm: ....
3pm: ....
4pm: ....
5pm: ....
6pm: ....
7pm: ....
8pm: ....
9pm: ....
10pm: ....

"One cannot think well, love well, sleep well, if one has not dined well."

VIRGINIA WOOLF

End of day check-in

WHAT WENT WELL TODAY?

HOW CAN I IMPROVE TOMORROW?

THREE THINGS I AM GRATEFUL FOR TODAY

TODAY I'VE FELT...

Tuesday

DATE:

TOP 3 PRIORITIES:

1. ....
....
....

2. ....
....
....

3. ....
....
....

HABIT TRACKER:

- ☐ ....
- ☐ ....
- ☐ ....
- ☐ ....
- ☐ ....

DAILY INTENTION:

8am: ....

9am: ....

10am: ....

11am: ....

12pm: ....

1pm: ....

2pm: ....

3pm: ....

4pm: ....

5pm: ....

6pm: ....

7pm: ....

8pm: ....

9pm: ....

10pm: ....

*"Food for the body is not enough.
There must be food for the soul."*

DOROTHY DAY

End of day check-in

WHAT WENT WELL TODAY?

HOW CAN I IMPROVE TOMORROW?

THREE THINGS I AM GRATEFUL FOR TODAY

TODAY I'VE FELT...

Wednesday

DATE:

DAILY INTENTION:

TOP 3 PRIORITIES:

1. ....
....
....

2. ....
....
....

3. ....
....
....

HABIT TRACKER:

☐ ....
☐ ....
☐ ....
☐ ....
☐ ....

8am: ....
9am: ....
10am: ....
11am: ....
12pm: ....
1pm: ....
2pm: ....
3pm: ....
4pm: ....
5pm: ....
6pm: ....
7pm: ....
8pm: ....
9pm: ....
10pm: ....

"Food is your body's fuel. Without fuel, your body wants to shut down."

KEN HILL

End of day check-in

WHAT WENT WELL TODAY?

HOW CAN I IMPROVE TOMORROW?

THREE THINGS I AM GRATEFUL FOR TODAY

TODAY I'VE FELT...

Thursday

DATE:

DAILY INTENTION:

TOP 3 PRIORITIES:

1. ....
   ....
   ....

2. ....
   ....
   ....

3. ....
   ....
   ....

HABIT TRACKER:

☐ ....
☐ ....
☐ ....
☐ ....
☐ ....

8am: ....
9am: ....
10am: ....
11am: ....
12pm: ....
1pm: ....
2pm: ....
3pm: ....
4pm: ....
5pm: ....
6pm: ....
7pm: ....
8pm: ....
9pm: ....
10pm: ....

"I know once people get connected to real food, they never change back."

ALICE WATERS

End of day check-in

WHAT WENT WELL TODAY?

HOW CAN I IMPROVE TOMORROW?

THREE THINGS I AM GRATEFUL FOR TODAY

TODAY I'VE FELT...

Friday

DATE:

TOP 3 PRIORITIES:

1. ....
....
....

2. ....
....
....

3. ....
....
....

HABIT TRACKER:

☐ ....
☐ ....
☐ ....
☐ ....
☐ ....

DAILY INTENTION:

8am: ....
9am: ....
10am: ....
11am: ....
12pm: ....
1pm: ....
2pm: ....
3pm: ....
4pm: ....
5pm: ....
6pm: ....
7pm: ....
8pm: ....
9pm: ....
10pm: ....

" Life is too short for self-hatred and celery sticks."

MARILYN WANN

End of day check-in

WHAT WENT WELL TODAY?

HOW CAN I IMPROVE TOMORROW?

THREE THINGS I AM GRATEFUL FOR TODAY

TODAY I'VE FELT...

Weekend

DATE:

TOP 3 PRIORITIES:

1. ....

....

....

2. ....

....

....

3. ....

....

....

HABIT TRACKER:

☐ ....

☐ ....

☐ ....

☐ ....

☐ ....

WEEKEND INTENTION:

9am: ....

10am; ....

11am: ....

12pm: ....

1pm: ....

2pm: ....

3pm: ....

4pm: ....

5pm: ....

6pm: ....

7pm: ....

8pm: ....

9pm: ....

10pm; ....

" You don't need a silver fork to eat good food."

PAUL PRUDHOMME

Weekend

DATE:

3 THINGS I AM GRATEFUL FOR THIS WEEKEND:

1. ....

....

....

2. ....

....

....

3. ....

....

....

9am:	....
10am:	....
11am:	....
12pm:	....
1pm:	....
2pm:	....
3pm:	....
4pm:	....
5pm:	....
6pm:	....
7pm:	....
8pm:	....
9pm:	....
10pm:	....

HABIT TRACKER:

☐ ....

☐ ....

☐ ....

☐ ....

☐ ....

THIS WEEKEND I'VE FELT...

☺ ☐ ☐ ☐ ☐ ☐ ☹

WEEK NINE: FUEL YOUR BODY AND MIND
End of week check-in

HOW DID THE 30 PLANT-BASED FOODS CHALLENGE GO?

HOW CAN I CONTINUE TO FUEL MY BODY BETTER?

WHAT ELSE DID I LEARN?

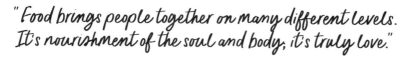

"Food brings people together on many different levels. It's nourishment of the soul and body, it's truly love."

GIADA DE LAURENTIIS

WHAT WERE MY TOP 5 ACHIEVEMENTS THIS WEEK?

WHAT THINGS MADE ME HAPPY THIS WEEK?

HOW WILL I MAKE NEXT WEEK AMAZING?

Week Ten
Practise Yoga

Whether you're brand new to yoga or been doing it for years, this week we're going to bring our minds and bodies together with this powerful practice.

Bringing Mind and Body Together with Yoga

The first yoga class I ever went to I nearly turned around and walked straight back out. Everyone had clearly been doing it for a lot longer than me and I felt embarrassed when I couldn't hold myself in the Downward Dog position. I gave up after my first few classes, resigning myself to the fact it just 'wasn't for me'. The instructor was too fast, I had no balance or strength, and I felt like a failure.

Fast forward a couple of years and I decided to start up yoga once again, this time online. I felt more comfortable not in a class full of people, but I still felt frustrated that my strength and balance was so off. I knew I enjoyed the mental health benefits of the practice, however, so I persevered. I wobbled, I struggled to get into positions, I fell over (countless times), and I kept going. You see, if you're new to yoga, then it can feel like you'll never 'get it' or that it's too hard. But, as I always say to people just starting out, you'd never expect to run a marathon without any practise so why do you expect so much of yourself from yoga?

This week, whether you're brand new to yoga or already enjoy the benefits, we're going to bring our minds and bodies together with this powerful practice. And remember, if you wobble or fall, get back onto your mat and keep going. I promise the pay-off will be so worth it.

WHY YOGA IS SO POWERFUL FOR THE BODY AND MIND

The reason I wanted to get into yoga in the first place was that I'd heard just how powerful it could be to improve your body and mind. In fact, there have now been countless studies into this ancient practice and the benefits that come with it. These include:

* Builds strength and flexibility

* Improves your posture

* Promotes better bone health and blood flow

* Can reduce blood pressure and improve heart health

* Increases serotonin levels (happy hormone) and reduces cortisol (stress hormone)

* Helps you remain focused

* Can promote better sleep and relaxation

* Helps you breathe deeper and become more mindful – which we already know all of the benefits of!

And many, many more that I'd need a whole other book to fit them all in!

GETTING STARTED AND IMPROVING YOUR YOGA PRACTICE

As I mentioned before, when I first started yoga I just thought it wasn't for me. However, I realised that like any kind of movement, I was going to need to practise. This week, I'd like you to focus on what you think yoga is and what it means to you; there's space in your planner for this too. Even if you consider yourself an expert at the practice, it's still important to check in and ask yourself why you do it.

On your online dashboard, you'll find three yoga lessons and an introduction from our incredible yoga teachers, Becky and Toma. There is one very basic lesson, a beginner's lesson, and an intermediate lesson. Depending on your skill level, I want you to pick the lesson that best works for you and practise it between 2-4 times. The same video, on repeat. After the first time you complete the lesson, write down how it made you feel and give yourself a score out of 10 for how you think it went. After you complete the lesson again, do the same thing – up to four times this week. If you are an expert, you can do more, but we don't want anyone feeling achy or sore!

What I want you to see is that every time you complete a lesson, you are improving. By repeating the same flow, you'll be able to see where you have improved. Imagine it's like a dance routine. You don't just do one dance class and then move on to another routine! You practise until you've got the steps right, before moving on.

If you wobble, fall over, or have to sit on the mat for some of it, just know that this is perfectly normal. Write that down in your planner, and at the end of the week make a note of how it has gone. You can then keep practising the same class until you're happy to move on to the next.

Yoga really did change my life and once I realised that it's not a competition, and that it's all about moving your body within your own limitations, it all fell into place for me. The mind and body benefits that come from yoga are worth wobbling on the mat a few times, trust me!

ONLINE RESOURCES FOR WEEK 10

* Video: A brief introduction from Toma and Becky

* Video: A 30-minute back to basics lesson with Becky

* Video: A 30-minute beginner's lesson with Becky

* Video: A 60-minute intermediate lesson with Toma

www.theantiburnoutclub.com/journal

Week Ten: Practise Yoga

What do you think yoga is? What does it mean to you? What do you think the benefits are?

....

....

....

....

Use this space to keep track of your thoughts after completing just one of the yoga lessons 2–4 times and mark yourself out of 10.

ATTEMPT 1 NOTES   ....

....

HOW DID IT GO? ...... /10

ATTEMPT 2 NOTES   ....

....

HOW DID IT GO? ...... /10

ATTEMPT 3 NOTES   ....

....

HOW DID IT GO? ...... /10

ATTEMPT 4 NOTES   ....

....

HOW DID IT GO? ...... /10

Remember to pick just one class and repeat this up to four times this week, based on your yoga experience!

WEEK COMMENCING:

ONE BIG GOAL FOR THE WEEK:

THIS WEEK WILL BE AMAZING IF I ALSO ACHIEVE...

1. ....
   ....

2. ....
   ....

3. ....
   ....

4. ....
   ....

5. ....
   ....

IMPORTANT THINGS TO REMEMBER THIS WEEK:

Monday:

Tuesday:

Wednesday:

Thursday:

Friday:

Saturday:

Sunday:

NOTES FOR THIS WEEK:

Monday

DATE:

DAILY INTENTION:

TOP 3 PRIORITIES:

1. ....

   ....

   ....

2. ....

   ....

   ....

3. ....

   ....

   ....

HABIT TRACKER:

☐ ....

☐ ....

☐ ....

☐ ....

☐ ....

8am: ....

9am: ....

10am: ....

11am: ....

12pm: ....

1pm: ....

2pm: ....

3pm: ....

4pm: ....

5pm: ....

6pm: ....

7pm: ....

8pm: ....

9pm: ....

10pm: ....

"Yoga is the journey of the self,
through the self, to the self."

THE BHAGAVAD GITA

End of day check-in

WHAT WENT WELL TODAY?

HOW CAN I IMPROVE TOMORROW?

THREE THINGS I AM GRATEFUL FOR TODAY

TODAY I'VE FELT...

Tuesday

DATE:

TOP 3 PRIORITIES:

1. ....
....
....

2. ....
....
....

3. ....
....
....

8am: ....
9am: ....
10am: ....
11am: ....
12pm: ....
1pm: ....
2pm: ....
3pm: ....
4pm: ....
5pm: ....
6pm: ....
7pm: ....
8pm: ....
9pm: ....
10pm: ....

HABIT TRACKER:

☐ ....
☐ ....
☐ ....
☐ ....
☐ ....

" In truth, yoga doesn't take
time - it gives time."

GANGA WHITE

End of day check-in

WHAT WENT WELL TODAY?

HOW CAN I IMPROVE TOMORROW?

THREE THINGS I AM GRATEFUL FOR TODAY

TODAY I'VE FELT...

Wednesday

DATE:

DAILY INTENTION:

TOP 3 PRIORITIES:

1. ....
   ....
   ....

2. ....
   ....
   ....

3. ....
   ....
   ....

HABIT TRACKER:

☐ ....
☐ ....
☐ ....
☐ ....
☐ ....

8am: ....
9am: ....
10am: ....
11am: ....
12pm: ....
1pm: ....
2pm: ....
3pm: ....
4pm: ....
5pm: ....
6pm: ....
7pm: ....
8pm: ....
9pm: ....
10pm: ....

*"Calming the mind is yoga.
Not just standing on the head."*

SWAMI SATCHIDANANDA

End of day check-in

WHAT WENT WELL TODAY?

HOW CAN I IMPROVE TOMORROW?

THREE THINGS I AM GRATEFUL FOR TODAY

TODAY I'VE FELT...

Thursday

DATE:

DAILY INTENTION:

TOP 3 PRIORITIES:

1. ....

   ....

   ....

2. ....

   ....

   ....

3. ....

   ....

   ....

8am: ....

9am: ....

10am: ....

11am: ....

12pm: ....

1pm: ....

2pm: ....

3pm: ....

4pm: ....

5pm: ....

6pm: ....

7pm: ....

8pm: ....

9pm: ....

10pm: ....

HABIT TRACKER:

☐ ....

☐ ....

☐ ....

☐ ....

☐ ....

" Yoga means addition. Addition of energy, strength and beauty to body, mind and soul."

AMIT RAY

End of day check-in

WHAT WENT WELL TODAY?

HOW CAN I IMPROVE TOMORROW?

THREE THINGS I AM GRATEFUL FOR TODAY

TODAY I'VE FELT...

Friday

DATE:

TOP 3 PRIORITIES:

1. ....

....

....

2. ....

....

....

3. ....

....

....

HABIT TRACKER:

☐ ....

☐ ....

☐ ....

☐ ....

☐ ....

DAILY INTENTION:

8am: ....

9am: ....

10am: ....

11am: ....

12pm: ....

1pm: ....

2pm: ....

3pm: ....

4pm: ....

5pm: ....

6pm: ....

7pm: ....

8pm: ....

9pm: ....

10pm: ....

*"Yoga does not just change the
way we see things, it transforms
the person who sees."*

B.K.S. IYENGAR

End of day check-in

WHAT WENT WELL TODAY?

HOW CAN I IMPROVE TOMORROW?

THREE THINGS I AM GRATEFUL FOR TODAY

TODAY I'VE FELT...

Weekend

DATE:

WEEKEND INTENTION:

TOP 3 PRIORITIES:

1. ....
   ....
   ....

2. ....
   ....
   ....

3. ....
   ....
   ....

HABIT TRACKER:

☐ ....
☐ ....
☐ ....
☐ ....
☐ ....

9am: ....
10am; ....
11am: ....
12pm: ....
1pm: ....
2pm: ....
3pm: ....
4pm: ....
5pm: ....
6pm: ....
7pm: ....
8pm: ....
9pm: ....
10pm; ....

" Yoga begins right where I am
- not where I was yesterday
or where I long to be."

LINDA SPARROWE

Weekend

DATE:

3 THINGS I AM GRATEFUL FOR THIS WEEKEND:

1. ....

....

....

2. ....

....

....

3. ....

....

....

9am: ....

10am: ....

11am: ....

12pm: ....

1pm: ....

2pm: ....

3pm: ....

4pm: ....

5pm: ....

6pm: ....

7pm: ....

8pm: ....

9pm: ....

10pm: ....

HABIT TRACKER:

☐ ....

☐ ....

☐ ....

☐ ....

☐ ....

THIS WEEKEND I'VE FELT...

☺ ☐ ☐ ☐ ☐ ☐ ☹

End of week check-in

HOW DID REPEATING THE SAME YOGA LESSON GO THIS WEEK?

HOW CAN I IMPROVE MY YOGA PRACTICE OVER TIME?

WHAT ELSE DID I LEARN?

"The very heart of yoga practice is 'abhyasa', steady effort in the direction you want to go."

SALLY KEMPTON

WHAT WERE MY TOP 5 ACHIEVEMENTS THIS WEEK?

WHAT THINGS MADE ME HAPPY THIS WEEK?

HOW WILL I MAKE NEXT WEEK AMAZING?

Week Eleven
Get More Sleep

Getting enough rest can have such a huge positive
impact on our physical and mental well-being,
and this week I'm going to help you switch off!

Getting More Sleep

One of the biggest factors in our mental and physical health is sleep. If we don't get enough sleep then we're more likely to feel stressed, anxious, depressed, want to overeat, not want to move our bodies, find it hard to concentrate, get grotty, and the list goes on and on. So, as we get closer to the end of these 12 weeks, I want us to spend a week concentrating on the importance of rest.

Modern technology has made it hard for us to switch off and is playing a huge part in the rise of insomnia and sleepless nights. When we feel overwhelmed, it can feel almost impossible to get a good night's sleep which then leads to all of the issues mentioned above. This week, we're going to focus on getting more sleep and how to switch off, but that's not all. For your Week 11 resources, I've brought in the absolutely amazing Dr. Charlie Moult, who is the breath work teacher for The Anti-Burnout Club. Charlie is going to walk you through an introduction to breath work and how powerful it can be for a range of things like sleep, stress and anxiety. You'll then find a quick breath work session that's perfect for before bed.

THE IMPORTANCE OF REST

As already mentioned, getting enough rest is imperative for both our physical and mental health. According to a recent survey, 36% of people struggle to get to sleep on a weekly basis with women struggling the most. The National Sleep Foundation found that adults should be getting around 7-9 hours of sleep a day, but most of us can admit that can be a struggle!

When we don't get enough rest, it can lead to short-term problems such as:

* Impaired memory and lack of alertness
* Reduced quality of life
* The urge to eat more, exercise less
* Heightened stress and anxiety

Ongoing stress and reduced quality of life can also have a longer-term negative impact on our overall well-being. So, the key to feeling good is getting enough rest!

WHAT TO DO WHEN YOUR MIND WON'T SWITCH OFF

It's all well and good me telling you that you need more sleep, but many of us struggle to switch our minds off at night. Research has shown that trying to fall asleep has become more of an issue as our reliance on technology grows, and it makes perfect sense. As we saw during the Unplug Yourself week, many of us use our phones before bed and this can have a negative impact on how easy it is to fall asleep.

Luckily, we have already covered some pretty incredible lessons to help make it easier to switch your mind off before bed. Unplugging, meditation, mindfulness, yoga, and even the food we eat can make it easier to drift off.

The best piece of advice I can give you is to find an evening routine that works for you. In your planner this week, I want you to start building a routine for before bed that will help you unwind and switch off. In the online resources, you'll find an article that will help you find the perfect wind-down evening routine.

Go through this and remember to add one little thing at a time. Just as we do with everything, especially habits, we need to build slowly. So, start by using what you learnt from the Unplug Yourself week to get less screen time before bed. You could then try a short meditation or yoga session to help you unwind. Slowly but surely, this evening routine will make it much easier for you to switch off and get more rest.

BREATHING FOR SLEEP

As mentioned, I've roped in the wonderful Charlie to provide you with a breath work session for this week. Breath work is an extremely powerful tool with a whole range of benefits (some of which Charlie discusses in her introduction). However, I have found it one of the most helpful methods to switch off and get better sleep at the end of the day.

Conscious breathing activates the parasympathetic nervous system, which can bring us into a more relaxed state and slow our heart rate. This can then make it easier to not only fall asleep but stay asleep too!

IF ALL ELSE FAILS, POWER NAP!

For some of us, trying to get enough sleep all at once is practically impossible. Perhaps that's due to other responsibilities, long shifts at work, or being a parent. If this is the case, you need the humble power nap.

I am a huge advocate of power napping when and wherever you can. As long as it's done right, the benefits are immense. The key is to try and squeeze in around 10-20 minutes of uninterrupted shut-eye, making sure it's not too late in the day. I've included the ultimate guide to power naps with your resources so you can nap like a pro.

Enjoy a more restful week and I'll see you for our last lesson next week...

ONLINE RESOURCES FOR WEEK 11

* Article: Creating a wind-down evening routine

* Article: The ultimate guide to power naps

* Video: Charlie introduces breath work

* Video: Breath work for sleep with Charlie

www.theantiburnoutclub.com/journal

Week Eleven: Get More Sleep

How do you feel when you don't get enough sleep? What impact do you think it has on your health and well-being?

....

....

....

....

....

....

After reading the online resource 'Creating a Wind-Down Evening Routine' use this space to write down your new before-bed routine.

THE FIRST WEEK I WILL...

....

....

NEXT WEEK I WILL ADD...

....

....

OTHER HABITS I WILL SLOWLY INTRODUCE...

....

....

Don't forget to take it step by step. Don't try overhauling your whole evening routine at once!

WEEK COMMENCING:

ONE BIG GOAL FOR THE WEEK:

THIS WEEK WILL BE AMAZING IF I ALSO ACHIEVE...

1. ....
   ....

2. ....
   ....

3. ....
   ....

4. ....
   ....

5. ....
   ....

IMPORTANT THINGS TO REMEMBER THIS WEEK:

Monday:

Tuesday:

Wednesday:

Thursday:

Friday:

Saturday:

Sunday:

NOTES FOR THIS WEEK:

Monday

DATE:

DAILY INTENTION:

TOP 3 PRIORITIES:

1.
_____
_____
_____

2.
_____
_____
_____

3.
_____
_____
_____

HABIT TRACKER:

☐ _____
☐ _____
☐ _____
☐ _____
☐ _____

8am: _____
9am: _____
10am: _____
11am: _____
12pm: _____
1pm: _____
2pm: _____
3pm: _____
4pm: _____
5pm: _____
6pm: _____
7pm: _____
8pm: _____
9pm: _____
10pm: _____

"Happiness consists of getting enough sleep. Just that, nothing more."

ROBERT A. HEINLEIN

End of day check-in

WHAT WENT WELL TODAY?

HOW CAN I IMPROVE TOMORROW?

THREE THINGS I AM GRATEFUL FOR TODAY

TODAY I'VE FELT...

Tuesday

DATE:

DAILY INTENTION:

TOP 3 PRIORITIES:

1. ....
....
....

2. ....
....
....

3. ....
....
....

8am: ....
9am: ....
10am: ....
11am: ....
12pm: ....
1pm: ....
2pm: ....
3pm: ....
4pm: ....
5pm: ....
6pm: ....
7pm: ....
8pm: ....
9pm: ....
10pm: ....

HABIT TRACKER:

☐ ....
☐ ....
☐ ....
☐ ....
☐ ....

" A well-spent day brings happy sleep."

LEONARDO DA VINCI

End of day check-in

WHAT WENT WELL TODAY?

HOW CAN I IMPROVE TOMORROW?

THREE THINGS I AM GRATEFUL FOR TODAY

TODAY I'VE FELT...

Wednesday

DATE:

TOP 3 PRIORITIES:

1. ....
   ....
   ....

2. ....
   ....
   ....

3. ....
   ....
   ....

HABIT TRACKER:

☐ ....
☐ ....
☐ ....
☐ ....
☐ ....

8am: ....
9am: ....
10am: ....
11am: ....
12pm: ....
1pm: ....
2pm: ....
3pm: ....
4pm: ....
5pm: ....
6pm: ....
7pm: ....
8pm: ....
9pm: ....
10pm: ....

"Sleep is the golden chain that ties health and our bodies together."

THOMAS DEKKER

End of day check-in

WHAT WENT WELL TODAY?

HOW CAN I IMPROVE TOMORROW?

THREE THINGS I AM GRATEFUL FOR TODAY

TODAY I'VE FELT...

Thursday

DATE:

TOP 3 PRIORITIES:

1. ....

....

....

2. ....

....

....

3. ....

....

....

HABIT TRACKER:

☐ ....

☐ ....

☐ ....

☐ ....

☐

DAILY INTENTION:

8am: ....

9am: ....

10am: ....

11am: ....

12pm: ....

1pm: ....

2pm: ....

3pm: ....

4pm: ....

5pm: ....

6pm: ....

7pm: ....

8pm: ....

9pm: ....

10pm: ....

"When the going gets tough, the tough take a nap."

TOM HODGKINSON

End of day check-in

WHAT WENT WELL TODAY?

HOW CAN I IMPROVE TOMORROW?

THREE THINGS I AM GRATEFUL FOR TODAY

TODAY I'VE FELT...

Friday

DATE:

TOP 3 PRIORITIES:

1. ....
....
....

2. ....
....
....

3. ....
....
....

HABIT TRACKER:

☐ ....
☐ ....
☐ ....
☐ ....
☐ ....

DAILY INTENTION:

8am: ....
9am: ....
10am: ....
11am: ....
12pm: ....
1pm: ....
2pm: ....
3pm: ....
4pm: ....
5pm: ....
6pm: ....
7pm: ....
8pm: ....
9pm: ....
10pm: ....

"No day is so bad it can't
be fixed with a nap."

CARRIE SNOW

End of day check-in

WHAT WENT WELL TODAY?

HOW CAN I IMPROVE TOMORROW?

THREE THINGS I AM GRATEFUL FOR TODAY

TODAY I'VE FELT...

Weekend

DATE:

WEEKEND INTENTION:

TOP 3 PRIORITIES:

1.

2.

3.

HABIT TRACKER:

☐
☐
☐
☐
☐

9am:
10am:
11am:
12pm:
1pm:
2pm:
3pm:
4pm:
5pm:
6pm:
7pm:
8pm:
9pm:
10pm:

"The best bridge between despair and hope is a good night's sleep."

E. JOSEPH COSSMAN

Weekend

DATE:

3 THINGS I AM GRATEFUL FOR THIS WEEKEND:

1. ....

....

....

2. ....

....

....

3. ....

....

....

9am: ....

10am: ....

11am: ....

12pm: ....

1pm: ....

2pm: ....

3pm: ....

4pm: ....

5pm: ....

6pm: ....

7pm: ....

8pm: ....

9pm: ....

10pm: ....

HABIT TRACKER:

☐ ....

☐ ....

☐ ....

☐ ....

☐ ....

THIS WEEKEND I'VE FELT...

WEEK ELEVEN: GET MORE SLEEP
End of week check-in

HOW DID I SLEEP THIS WEEK?

HOW CAN I MAKE SURE I CAN GET BETTER SLEEP GOING FORWARD?

WHAT ELSE DID I LEARN?

> *"Let her sleep, for when she wakes, she will shake the world."*

NAPOLEON BONAPARTE

WHAT WERE MY TOP 5 ACHIEVEMENTS THIS WEEK?

WHAT THINGS MADE ME HAPPY THIS WEEK?

HOW WILL I MAKE NEXT WEEK AMAZING?

Week Twelve
Celebrate Your Success

You're on the final week of this 12-week journey and it's time to celebrate just how far you've come – and plan what's next!

Celebrating Our Successes

It's the final week of this 12-week journey and I have one thing to say to you: 'You've made it'! I know that some weeks may have felt easier than others, and you may have even experienced some setbacks along the way – this might be week 52 instead of week 12 for you! However, the important thing is that you've made it through. So, the focus this week is on celebrating our successes and why it's so important to do so.

Don't forget to check the resources to go with this lesson, as I don my party hat and celebrate your success and discuss how to continue with the incredible journey you've started.

WHY CELEBRATE OUR SUCCESS?

How many times have you said to yourself that you wanted to achieve something, did it (or at least gave it a really good shot) and then moved on to the next thing? I'll put my hands up and say I've lost count of the number of times I've done this myself! The issue is, when we don't celebrate how far we've come, we often feel left longing.

A quote that really resonates with me is: 'Remember when you wanted what you currently have?'. Think about it. Remember when you wanted that promotion or pay rise, you got it, and then you instantly started working towards the next one. Or when you wanted that new pair of shoes or car or to go on holiday? You got those things and then you wanted something else.

It's called hedonic adaptation and while there's no way of stopping it from happening, there is a way of slowing it down – celebrating our successes! Being grateful for everything we have done, everything we've achieved, every time we tried our best, everything we have – just like we did back in Week 3 – can increase our levels of happiness and contentment for much longer than usual.

LOOKING BACK OVER THE 12 WEEKS

So, let's look at what you have achieved over the last 12 weeks. We have covered so much, from setting intentions and creating better habits, through to moving our bodies more, yoga, and even committing to Random Acts of Kindness.

We have learnt a whole deal about our health, our well-being and ourselves. We know how to rest better, fuel our bodies better, and all about the joys of unplugging. We may not have filled in our planner every day or every week, or met our goal or intentions each time, but what we have done is gone on a journey that has given us time to ourselves, to reflect and to be kinder to ourselves.

KEEPING THE MOMENTUM GOING

Now that we've got to the end of the 12 weeks, what's next for you? Getting the ball rolling was the hardest part of this whole experience, so keeping that momentum going is super important! Here are some top tips to make sure you can keep these changes past the 12 weeks:

* **Go back and look through each lesson again, working out what other areas you could work on:** Perhaps you could unplug a little longer, try a harder yoga class, or add more Random Acts of Kindness into your weeks.

* **Making small, gradual changes:** Just like we learnt at the very beginning with our habits, making small changes is the key to success. How did you get on with adding new habits every four weeks? Is it time to add another positive habit?

* **Continue your learning:** It's okay if you didn't get through all of the extra resources that come with this journal – there are a lot! However, to keep the momentum going, go back through the lessons to tick off the ones you've missed.

* **Stay with us:** If you'd like to extend your learning beyond these 12 weeks, then there's a special offer for you to join The Anti-Burnout Club for even more lessons, challenges, classes, recipes and more.

* **Get an accountability buddy.** I hope you've found this journal the perfect accountability buddy for the last 12 weeks, and now it's time to rope in someone else! If you're a member of The ABC then you'll find some wonderful members of the community to pair up with – or ask friends, family members and loved ones to keep you accountable to your new lifestyle.

Finally, I just wanted to say a huge congratulations for working your way through these 12 weeks. Sticking to something for this length of time can feel like a huge task in itself sometimes, and the fact you've made it to the end deserves the biggest pat on the back that you can give yourself. Spend this week reflecting, planning ahead, and then celebrate!

ONLINE RESOURCES FOR WEEK 12

* Video: Congratulations and reflections with Bex

* Article: What's next? Continuing your journey

www.theantiburnoutclub.com/journal

Week Twelve: Celebrate Your Success

What have been your biggest successes over the last 12 weeks? How will you celebrate and reward yourself?

✳ ....

✳ ....

✳ ....

✳ ....

✳ ....

✳ ....

What tools are you going to put in place to keep the momentum going?

....

....

....

....

I have a couple more goodies for you before you close this journal for the last time – so make sure you read all the way until the end this week!

WEEK COMMENCING:

ONE BIG GOAL FOR THE WEEK:

THIS WEEK WILL BE AMAZING IF I ALSO ACHIEVE...

1. ....
....

2. ....
....

3. ....
....

4. ....
....

5. ....
....

IMPORTANT THINGS TO REMEMBER THIS WEEK:

Monday:

Tuesday:

Wednesday:

Thursday:

Friday:

Saturday:

Sunday:

NOTES FOR THIS WEEK:

Monday

DATE:

DAILY INTENTION:

TOP 3 PRIORITIES:

1. ....

   ....

   ....

2. ....

   ....

   ....

3. ....

   ....

   ....

HABIT TRACKER:

☐ ....

☐ ....

☐ ....

☐ ....

☐ ....

8am: ....
9am: ....
10am: ....
11am: ....
12pm: ....
1pm: ....
2pm: ....
3pm: ....
4pm: ....
5pm: ....
6pm: ....
7pm: ....
8pm: ....
9pm: ....
10pm: ....

"Success is the sum of small efforts - repeated day in and day out."

ROBERT COLLIER

End of day check-in

WHAT WENT WELL TODAY?

HOW CAN I IMPROVE TOMORROW?

THREE THINGS I AM GRATEFUL FOR TODAY

TODAY I'VE FELT...

Tuesday

DATE:

DAILY INTENTION:

TOP 3 PRIORITIES:

1. ....

   ....

   ....

2. ....

   ....

   ....

3. ....

   ....

   ....

8am: ....

9am: ....

10am: ....

11am: ....

12pm: ....

1pm: ....

2pm: ....

3pm: ....

4pm: ....

5pm: ....

6pm: ....

7pm: ....

8pm: ....

9pm: ....

10pm: ....

HABIT TRACKER:

☐ ....

☐ ....

☐ ....

☐ ....

☐ ....

" In my experience, there's no secret to accomplishing almost any goal worth pursuing."

LAUREN GRAHAM

End of day check-in

WHAT WENT WELL TODAY?

HOW CAN I IMPROVE TOMORROW?

THREE THINGS I AM GRATEFUL FOR TODAY

TODAY I'VE FELT...

Wednesday

DATE:

DAILY INTENTION:

TOP 3 PRIORITIES:

1. ....

....

....

2. ....

....

....

3. ....

....

....

HABIT TRACKER:

- ☐ ....
- ☐ ....
- ☐ ....
- ☐ ....
- ☐ ....

8am: ....

9am: ....

10am: ....

11am: ....

12pm: ....

1pm: ....

2pm: ....

3pm: ....

4pm: ....

5pm: ....

6pm: ....

7pm: ....

8pm: ....

9pm: ....

10pm: ....

"Everyone is trying to accomplish something big, not realising that life is made up of little things."

FRANK A. CLARK

End of day check-in

WHAT WENT WELL TODAY?

HOW CAN I IMPROVE TOMORROW?

THREE THINGS I AM GRATEFUL FOR TODAY

TODAY I'VE FELT...

Thursday

DATE:

TOP 3 PRIORITIES:

1. ....
....
....

2. ....
....
....

3. ....
....
....

HABIT TRACKER:

☐ ....
☐ ....
☐ ....
☐ ....
☐ ....

DAILY INTENTION:

8am: ....
9am: ....
10am: ....
11am: ....
12pm: ....
1pm: ....
2pm: ....
3pm: ....
4pm: ....
5pm: ....
6pm: ....
7pm: ....
8pm: ....
9pm: ....
10pm: ....

" If you never had any bad
days, you would never have that
sense of accomplishment!"

ALY RAISMAN

End of day check-in

WHAT WENT WELL TODAY?

HOW CAN I IMPROVE TOMORROW?

THREE THINGS I AM GRATEFUL FOR TODAY

TODAY I'VE FELT...

Friday

DATE:

TOP 3 PRIORITIES:

1. ....
....
....

2. ....
....
....

3. ....
....
....

HABIT TRACKER:

☐ ....
☐ ....
☐ ....
☐ ....
☐ ....

DAILY INTENTION:

8am: ....
9am: ....
10am: ....
11am: ....
12pm: ....
1pm: ....
2pm: ....
3pm: ....
4pm: ....
5pm: ....
6pm: ....
7pm: ....
8pm: ....
9pm: ....
10pm: ....

" Lord knows, every day is not a
success, every year is not a success.
You have to celebrate the good."

REESE WITHERSPOON

End of day check-in

WHAT WENT WELL TODAY?

HOW CAN I IMPROVE TOMORROW?

THREE THINGS I AM GRATEFUL FOR TODAY

TODAY I'VE FELT...

Weekend

DATE:

WEEKEND INTENTION:

TOP 3 PRIORITIES:

1. ....

....

....

2. ....

....

....

3. ....

....

....

HABIT TRACKER:

☐ ....

☐ ....

☐ ....

☐ ....

☐ ....

9am: ....

10am: ....

11am: ....

12pm: ....

1pm: ....

2pm: ....

3pm: ....

4pm: ....

5pm: ....

6pm: ....

7pm: ....

8pm: ....

9pm: ....

10pm: ....

*"Every individual has within
their abilities the capability of
accomplishing extraordinary things."*

BRIAN TRACY

Weekend

DATE:

3 THINGS I AM GRATEFUL FOR THIS WEEKEND:

1. ....

....

....

2. ....

....

....

3. ....

....

....

9am: ....

10am: ....

11am: ....

12pm: ....

1pm: ....

2pm: ....

3pm: ....

4pm: ....

5pm: ....

6pm: ....

7pm: ....

8pm: ....

9pm: ....

10pm: ....

HABIT TRACKER:

☐ ....

☐ ....

☐ ....

☐ ....

☐ ....

THIS WEEKEND I'VE FELT...

☺ ☐ ☐ ☐ ☐ ☐ ☹

End of week check-in

HOW DID I REWARD MYSELF THIS WEEK FOR ALL I HAVE ACHIEVED?

WHAT ARE MY 3 KEY STEPS GOING FORWARD TO KEEP THE MOMENTUM?

WHAT ELSE DID I LEARN?

"The most beautiful things are not associated with money, they are memories and moments. If you don't celebrate those, they can pass you by."

ALEK WEK

WHAT WERE MY TOP 5 ACHIEVEMENTS THIS WEEK?

WHAT THINGS MADE ME HAPPY THIS WEEK?

HOW WILL I MAKE NEXT WEEK AMAZING?

You Did It! Some Final Notes from Bex

Wow, what a journey these 12 weeks have been. Before you close this journal for the last time, I have a couple of extra things for you...

DEAR ME...

The first is the My Final Reflection Letter. Here, I'd like you to write a note to yourself about how the last 12 weeks have gone. Be open and honest – no one is going to read it but you! Describe the journey you have been on and make a note of anything you particularly loved or anything you found difficult.

But most importantly, use it as a space to praise yourself for all of the work you have put in over the last 12 weeks. This is an amazing letter to come back to, perhaps in a month or two, to see how much has changed since then. Are you still working on your intentions? How are those habits coming along? Are you still proud of all your achievements? Come back to this letter at any time to remind yourself that you can do it (and you did)!

WHAT'S NEXT?

I briefly spoke about keeping the momentum going in the last week of the journal, so now is the perfect time to think about what's next. Perhaps you've discovered a love of yoga and want to start practising it more often? Maybe you want to keep expanding on those good habits or unplugging more often?

At the end of this journal, I have included two special offers to help you continue on your journey.

The first is a discount to access all the other resources in The Anti-Burnout Club member's area; including over 200 more lessons and recipes. We also run monthly challenges and courses, if you liked the structure of the last 12 weeks.

I have also included a discount for your next journal! If you want to keep the momentum going and loved having daily and weekly check-ins, then you can start this journal all over again from the beginning. Does it matter that you've already completed it once? Not at all! You can still gain a lot from the lessons and the structure.

A FINAL THANK YOU

Finally, wherever you go next in your wellness journey, I wanted to say a personal thank you from the bottom of my heart. Thank you for buying the journal, thank you for taking the time to learn and grow with me, and thank you for giving it your all.

Remember, this is a journey. The 12 weeks may be over, but you'll continue to grow and learn and flourish if you follow the Anti-Burnout principles.

I'd love to hear how it all went for you, so please do feel free to reach out.

I hope to see you again very soon.

Take care,

Bex x

My Final Reflection Letter

Dear .... (your name)

....

....

....

....

....

....

....

....

....

....

....

....

....

....

....

....

....

....

....

Further Reflection

Use this space for any notes, observations and feelings you want to record at the end of the process.

About Bex

Bex is a formerly burnt-out entrepreneur who closed down her marketing agency in September 2020, before launching The Anti-Burnout Club in January 2021. Having gone from being inherently stressed (and believing that's just how life was), she decided to study mindfulness and well-being before realising there was another way. She set up The Anti-Burnout Club in the hopes of making self-care more accessible, bringing together a range of incredible teachers and experts to provide lessons on everything from avoiding burnout through to self-confidence.

Bex lives in Tunbridge Wells, Kent with her husband Jake and two dogs, Chewy and Obi.

Acknowledgements

Firstly, I want to thank my incredible husband Jake who quashed every single bit of self-doubt I had about writing my first ever published piece of work. Jake, I couldn't have written a single word of this without your support and for telling me 'you CAN' every day.

Next, a huge thank you to Ame Verso who came to me with the idea for this journal and enabled me to think bigger than I ever had before. This journal literally wouldn't exist without you and I can't thank you enough for the faith you put in me, and for your patience.

Huge thanks to Sam Staddon for the wonderful layouts and cover – I can't believe it looks this good – I keep pinching myself! And to Jeni Chown and the team at David & Charles for their help in bringing this journal to life.

I can't forget the amazing team who help make The Anti-Burnout Club the safe and inspiring space that it is – some of whom you'll have met in this journal!

To Aga Kehinde, Anna Mapson, Becky Guest, Charlie Moult, Codie Wright, Coz Hutchinson, Emily Hyland, Gemma Curtis, Rachael Bond, Rebecca Spick and Toma Janultye-Stankevic.

To all of my friends and family who I know will likely buy this journal to see if their names are in it. Amy, Zanna, Georgia, Helena, Helen, Kate, Rose, Tiff, Corrina, George, Kat, I love you all.

Finally, my biggest thank you goes to every member of The Anti-Burnout Club community. I'd need pages and pages to express my gratitude to you all. YOU wrote this as much as I did.

About The Anti-Burnout Club

The Anti-Burnout Club is on a mission to make self-care more accessible! We have provided a platform of over 200 lessons and recipes, monthly challenges and courses, all designed to improve your overall well-being. We have lessons in:

* Yoga
* Pilates
* Meditation
* Mindfulness
* Breath work

* EFT (Tapping)
* Sleep stories
* CBT and other therapies
* Motivation

* Productivity
* Self-confidence and self-love
* And so much more...

THE **anti-burnout** CLUB

Exclusive Membership Offer

If you want to continue your journey with The ABC then login to your online resources where you will find an exclusive special offer for journal owners. Can't find the offer? Make sure you've signed up at https://theantiburnoutclub.com/journal with the code from the How to Use This Journal and Resources section. I hope to see you there!

Save 20% on Your Next Journal

Want to start all over again with the lessons? Or just want to use *The Anti-Burnout Journal* for the weekly and daily planners? Use the exclusive code below at https://theantiburnoutclub.com/shop to get 20% off your next journal (or two or four):

NEWJOURNALNEWME20

A DAVID AND CHARLES BOOK
© David and Charles, Ltd 2022

David and Charles is an imprint of David and Charles, Ltd
Suite A, Tourism House, Pynes Hill, Exeter, EX2 5WS

Text © Bex Spiller 2022
Layout © David and Charles, Ltd 2022

First published in the UK and USA in 2022

A catalogue record for this book is available from the British Library.

ISBN-13: 9781446309155 hardback

This book has been printed on paper from approved suppliers and
made from pulp from sustainable sources.

Printed in Turkey by Omur Printing and Packaging for:
David and Charles, Ltd
Suite A, Tourism House, Pynes Hill, Exeter, EX2 5WS

10 9 8 7 6 5 4 3 2

Publishing Director: Ame Verso
Managing Editor: Jeni Chown
Designer: Sam Staddon
Pre-Press Designer: Ali Stark
Illustrations: Marsala Digital
Production Manager: Beverley Richardson

David and Charles publishes high-quality books on a wide range of
subjects. For more information visit www.davidandcharles.com.

Share with us on social media using #dandcbooks and follow us on
Facebook and Instagram by searching for @dandcbooks.